THE BEGINNER'S GUIDE TO
RADIO CONTROL
SPORT FLYING

DOUGLAS R. PRATT

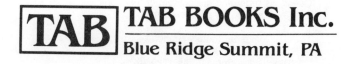

TAB TAB BOOKS Inc.
Blue Ridge Summit, PA

FIRST EDITION
THIRD PRINTING

Copyright © 1988 by TAB BOOKS Inc.
Printed in the United States of America

Library of Congress Cataloging in Publication Data

Pratt, Douglas R.
The beginner's guide to radio control sport flying.

Includes index.
1. Airplanes—Models—Radio control. I. Title.
TL770.P68 1988   629.133′134   88-2268
        ISBN 0-8306-9320-3 (pbk.)

TAB BOOKS Inc. offers software for
sale. For information and a catalog,
please contact TAB Software Department,
Blue Ridge Summit, PA 17294-0850.

Questions regarding the content of this book
should be addressed to:

Reader Inquiry Branch
TAB BOOKS Inc.
Blue Ridge Summit, PA 17294-0214

Contents

Introduction

AFTER ALL THESE YEARS, I'M STILL GENUINELY EX-cited by model airplanes of all kinds. I still rush to finish a model so I can fly, and I still frantically charge all my batteries when there's a forecast of good weather.

I wrote this book for the *average* RC flier—like me. There are plenty of books around for fliers who are zeroed in on one discipline or another. Even though I've built models since I was eight, I've never found *one* type of model to dominate my time and energy. There's just too much neat stuff around to ignore any of it.

I hope you enjoy reading this book; I enjoyed putting it together for you. I've tried to make it as useful as possible. In places where I've left things out, or not told as much as I probably should have, it's because I didn't have enough information. I figured it was better to not say anything than to put in stuff I wasn't sure of. There are undoubtedly mistakes in here; when something you read varies with your experience, please write and let me know. I'm always trying to learn.

An undertaking the size of this book is well-nigh impossible for one person. I had a lot of help. John Worth, Bob Underwood, Jeff Troy, Lou Ward, Vince Mankowski, and Chip Smith all helped with parts of the manuscript. Geoff Wheeler and George Zombakis of *Model Retailer* magazine lent me a lot of pictures. Thanks, folks, for making this better than it would have been.

I've been privileged to spend a lot of time with Bill Winter over the last few years. Editor of model magazines since the 1930s, author of more books than he can remember, and creator of friendly airplanes, Bill has been an inspiration and a delight. Thanks, Bill; let's go flying tomorrow.

Anyone who does something like this book had better have a supportive wife. My wife went out and bought a camera and taught herself to use a darkroom so we could get most of the pictures here. It would have been impossible without her, and she did a darned good job, too.

Thank you, Jennifer; this book is dedicated to you.

Chapter 1

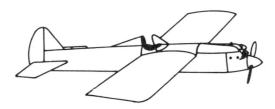

This Rewarding Hobby

AEROMODELING IS A UNIQUE ACTIVITY IN MANY ways. For one thing, it's both a hobby and a sport. The thrill of competition is there, and we can train for it like any other athletes. But the vast majority of us treat aeromodeling as a hobby. We do it for our own satisfaction. We build what strikes our fancy, fly as much as we please when we please, and if we get an occasional trophy or award along the way, so much the better. The activity itself is the reward most of us seek.

I wrote this book for the sport fliers among us. I'm a sport flier myself. I've built a lot of kits, run a lot of engines, charged a lot of radio systems, and done my share of crashing. I've flown almost every kind of model airplane, and listened to fliers who specialize in all the different types. Sure, I've found a few types that I enjoy more than others, but I remain fascinated by them all.

When I planned this book (and its companion volume, *The Advanced Guide to Radio Control Sport Flying*, TAB Book #3060), I tried to make it as useful as possible for the average flier like me.

There is no information here about how to hop up engines, or repair radios, or do other things that the average guy is too busy flying to do. There's plenty of information on how to tell what's wrong with your engine or radio, and advice on whether you should try to fix it yourself or send it back.

I've tried to cover many of the popular RC model kits in at least enough detail to give you an idea of whether or not you might like to build one. In several of the chapters, I've picked one or two kits that represent the type of plane I'm talking about and gone into them in detail. You can gather a lot of information about the other kits in this category from these discussions, not to mention building tricks and techniques that apply to many other models.

The Appendices at the back of the book contain a list of hobby manufacturers. This list doesn't cover every company in the industry, of course, but most of the important ones are there. Please note that you can almost always purchase these people's products at your local hobby shop. If your dealer hasn't got the item in stock, he can get it. Manufac-

1

turer addresses are included here so you can write to them for current catalogs and product information. If you're not lucky enough to have a hobby store near you, there are reputable mail-order firms listed in the same index.

You'll also find information on RC frequencies in the Appendices. Since the FCC approved new space for RC frequencies, the AMA has set regulations for gradually phasing in the new frequencies. You need to understand how this system works so that you know what frequencies are proper to use. It's not complicated, but it's important information. The information in the back of this book comes from the AMA Frequency Committee, and is up-to-date as of the date of publication. You can always get the latest information by writing to AMA's Technical Director, Bob Underwood, at the AMA address. A complete discussion of the Phase-In Plan is in Chapter 3.

THE MODEL INDUSTRY

I've been privileged to be involved in the hobby industry for a lot of years. Any industry is made up of people, and this industry is made up of a great bunch of people. To a man (or woman), they're truly excited about the products they make. They're anxious to tell you about their stuff, and they're eager to hear what *you* think.

Aeromodeling has a lot to offer those who participate. The consumer is closer to the cutting edge of technology in this business than almost any other field I can think of. Someone gets a good idea for a product and starts producing it. They might appear at a small booth at a trade show. Perhaps they sell a few items at shows, and that's as far as it goes. Sometimes the product takes off, and the entrepreneur finds his spare time taken up with his project. It can end with a thriving business, or the sale of the product to another manufacturer who adds it to their line. In any case, the consumer has a remarkable access to the companies who design, manufacture, and market the products they use.

DIVERSITY: AN AIRPLANE FOR EVERYONE

I've never quite figured out what people enjoy about putting together jigsaw puzzles. It's hard work

. . . and when you finish, you have the same picture that you saw on the cover of the box. I'm unimpressed.

Why not use the same skills and turn out an airplane? You're working in three dimensions, with balsa wood (which has always seemed like magical stuff to me) instead of printed cardboard. Most of all, what you get when you're done is capable of more magic yet: You can take it out and *fly* it.

If you're a fan of full-size planes, you can find something to fascinate you. Warbirds, classic aircraft, modern jetliners and fighters—you can be flying one in a matter of weeks. If it's the flight itself that fascinates you, you'll be able to experiment to your heart's content. One of my favorite planes was inherited from Bill Winter, a world-famous model designer. He and I have spent many pleasant hours discussing and trying minor changes to see how they affect its flight. Are you looking for relaxation? There's nothing in the world as relaxing as a slow, smooth-flying sailplane or Old-Timer making gentle turns on a sunny day. Speed, aerobatics, nostalgia, science—it's all here.

KEEPING UP: RC MAGAZINES

The model airplane world is lucky to have a wide range of magazines devoted to it. Without exception they are fine publications, well worth their cost. True fanatics subscribe to four or more magazines, and hoard them for their construction articles, kit reviews, and contest reports. Each of these magazines has a distinct character, appealing to different types of people. I read them all, and I'd like to describe them to you. I'll present them in alphabetical order so my own preferences aren't quite so obvious.

Flying Models. *Flying Models* magazine, published by Carstens Publications in New Jersey, is one of the oldest model magazines around. It traces its proud lineage back to the *Flying Aces* of the 1930s. The present-day *FM* is an interesting mix that covers the sport well. It's an "editorial sandwich," meaning that the ads are concentrated at the front and the back, with editorials and product reviews interspersed with the ads. The articles run through the middle pages, uninterrupted by ads, with plenty of pictures. Despite its title, *Flying Models* has an extensive RC boating section. Bob Aberle's excellent product review articles are worth the cost of an *FM* subscription. Their regular columns include an excellent Giant Scale series by Frank Costello, a scale column by acknowledged master Dave Platt, regular articles on control line flying, and engine reviews.

Model Airplane News. *Model Airplane News* is another magazine with a long and venerable history; they have been publishing for well over 50 years. The modern *MAN* is devoted entirely to RC coverage. It's a large, slick publication with a lot of color photos and eye-catching graphics. Two of my favorite features are the page of "Hints and Tips" by Jim Newman and Randy Randolph's advice for beginning modelers. You'll find plenty of product reviews, plus some very nice regular features on full-size aircraft.

Model Aviation. *Model Aviation* is the official publication of the AMA, and you get it as part of your membership. Since the AMA covers all model flying activity, you'll find regular columns in *Model Aviation* for every category of model—RC, free flight, and control line. You'll also find a complete calendar of AMA-sanctioned contests, reports on contest rules and AMA affairs in the monthly AMA News section, and several pages of brief product reviews. There are always at least two construction articles, and full-size plans are available.

Model Builder. *Model Builder* magazine is one of the most complete model publications in the world. It regularly covers free flight and control line models as well as RC, and has been one of the major reasons for the growth of Peanut Scale. There's often a full-size Peanut plan published in the center-spread. *MB* is always interesting; the personality of Editor Bill Northrup pervades it. Stu Richmond's "Engines of the World" column is an engine fancier's delight. Eloy Marez's regular "Electronics Corner" is another unique feature. *MB* is also home for Bill Hannan's monthly collection of cheery tidbits, "Hannan's Hangar." I never miss it.

Model Shopper. April 1987 saw the premiere of a new major model magazine called *Model Shopper.* Those of us who are into computers noticed the

similarity to a magazine called *Computer Shopper; Model Shopper* is tabloid-size with glossy covers. It sure stands out on a magazine rack. In fact, *MS* is published by a company that puts out three successful magazines for personal computer users.

The idea behind *Model Shopper* is to provide lots of current product information, along with commentary and articles about all kinds of models. RC is a big part of *MS*, but there's plenty of material on railroading, plastic models, and other kinds of model airplanes. It's going to be interesting to see how *Model Shopper* develops; it's certainly a different concept—and useful.

RC Modeler. The largest magazine in the model publishing business is *RC Modeler.* Just about everyone reads it, and just about all model companies advertise in it. With over 200 pages every month, there's no better way to keep up with new product releases. Ken Willard's "Sunday Flier" column is an institution to *RCM* readers, as is Don Lowe's "Flying Lowe" series. Clarence Lee's monthly column on model engines and regular engine review articles are absolutely invaluable.

RC Report. The newest star in the model magazine sky is a unique one. *RC Report* is a monthly magazine printed tabloid-style on newsprint. After less than a year of publishing, it's gained a strong reputation for its breezy style and "tell it like it is" product reviews. *RC Report* often has news items faster than the other magazines that take longer to produce and print. I've been very impressed with it, and I predict that they'll get bigger and better.

RC Video Magazine. *RC Video Magazine* is unique. It's published quarterly, and it's a magazine intended for model fliers, but instead of getting a printed magazine, you get a two-hour videotape. *RCVM* has been publishing for more than two years. It's professionally done by people who have won awards for their commercial video work. They send camera crews to model meets all over North America. *RCVM* also contains kit reviews and how-to articles. There are even advertisements. Rather than trying to do what the print magazines do, *RCVM* concentrates on things that work best in action. You'll find that there's too much to watch at

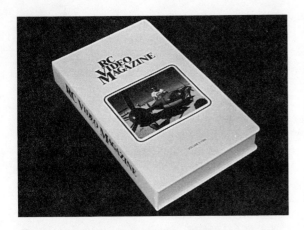

RC Video Magazine is a quarterly model magazine published on videotape instead of paper. Each issue contains features on model meets, kit reviews, how-to articles, and even advertisements. (Photo courtesy *Model Retailer* magazine)

one sitting; that's why so many clubs show parts of *RCVM* at their meetings. A four-issue subscription to *RC Video Magazine* costs around $100; individual copies cost around $35, and back issues never go out of print.

Scale RC Modeler. *Scale RC Modeler* is a bimonthly title that specializes in one of the most popular categories of RC. It contains more meet coverage than most other magazines; the pictures of contest-quality scale ships are always interesting. *SRCM* often features articles on full-size planes that make interesting modeling subjects. There are also plenty of scale kit reviews. They've recently begun a monthly series that takes an in-depth look at ready-to-fly scale models.

TRADE SHOWS

Ah, trade shows—Modelers' Meccas. They're held throughout the country each year, and the bigger ones attract modelers from around the world. Smaller shows are usually sponsored by clubs, and draw hundreds of modelers to see displays of new products and participate in swap shops and auctions.

The Toledo RC Show is the grandaddy of the RC trade shows. It's been held in the Toledo, Ohio, Sports Arena in April for over 30 years. Several hundred manufacturers set up display booths and sell their products; booth space is always at a premium.

Toledo is so central to the modeler's year that many manufacturers time new product releases for the show. As a result, you'll see prototypes and announcements of brand-new stuff at this show. The Arena is fairly small, and exhibitors complain about the limited facilities, but complaining or not, they're there. Toledo also has a very large swap shop area where you can dicker for anything from barely-repairable planes to precious antique engines.

The traditional beginning of the modeler's year is the International Modeler Show on the West Coast. IMS has been held for over 10 years in Pasadena, CA, the second weekend of January. It has grown steadily, and is now the major trade show for the California area. Because of the large number of modelers in the California area, manufacturer turnout is always high. IMS features some unique events, such as control line and RC exhibition flying by the famous Black Sheep Squadron right in the middle of the exhibit hall.

On the other coast, the surest sign of spring is the Westchester Radio Aero Modelers' show in White Plains, NY, just north of New York City. The WRAM show is almost as old as Toledo, and is just as important to the large concentration of modelers in the New York-New Jersey area. It's held every March, and features a large number of manufacturer exhibits. There's also a static model competition, where models in all categories are judged by a panel of experts. A large auction and several classes where youngsters learn to build free Delta Dart models add to the attraction.

The Pacific Northwest has developed its own major trade show, the Northwest Expo. It's held every February in Puyallup, WA, near Seattle. The NW Expo has grown rapidly; it serves an area where there are a lot of enthusiastic modelers, and the exhibitors are always pleased with the response. The facilities of the County Fairgrounds where the NW Expo is held are excellent; there's room for a car track and helicopter flying demos.

The newest major show on the calendar is the Chicago Model and Hobby Show. The Chicago Show is held every year in October or early November. It's organized and run by the Radio Control Hobbies Trade Association, a group of model manufacturers, distributors, and retailers. The show actually opens on Thursday, but the first two days are open to the trade only. It's become a major attraction for hobby store owners and buyers from all over the country. On Saturday, the fun begins; last year, well over 20,000 people visited the show over the weekend. The Chicago Show is heavily advertised, so many of the people who attend are looking at aeromodeling for the first time. Chicago area modelers show off their best in a large static exhibit.

If you can attend one of these shows, it will be an experience you'll never forget. There's no better way to taste the diversity of this hobby; you can find almost everything there. And the enthusiasm you'll feel from everyone, businessmen and customers alike, is bound to impress you. I've been going to these shows for almost 15 years, working both sides of the display tables, and I still get excited.

THE ACADEMY OF MODEL AERONAUTICS

The Academy of Model Aeronautics is the national organization of aeromodelers in the United States. In its 50-year history, it's grown to be the largest sport aviation organization in the world.

In a very real sense, aeromodeling as we know it wouldn't exist without the AMA. RC flying is just one example. When RC began, you had to pass a test and get an amateur radio license to do it. AMA worked to have the restrictions removed and more channels made available. Eventually the license requirement was changed so that an RC license was similar to a CB license. Then the license requirement was dropped completely. Finally, thanks to the efforts of the AMA Frequency Committee, the number of channels available for RC has increased from eight to 22, with more to come in the near future.

AMA is governed by an Executive Council that consists of District Vice Presidents elected from 11 districts around the U.S. There are also two nationally-elected officers, the President and the Executive Vice President. Elected officials serve three-year terms. AMA Headquarters in Reston, VA, is the main office. Presiding over Headquarters is Executive Director John Worth, who has had the job for well over 20 years. Mr. Worth has seen AMA

grow from one full-time secretary and some part-time help to a thriving operation with 45 employees.

AMA Insurance

The most obvious function of AMA is insurance. In the lawsuit-happy age we live in, an accident is very likely to result in legal action. Model clubs have even been sued for making noise. AMA members are covered by liability insurance while they are engaged in modeling activities. AMA-chartered clubs can extend that coverage to the person, governmental body, or company that owns their flying field. This has saved a lot of flying sites; well over 80 percent of the flying fields in the country would close if this insurance were unavailable.

AMA insurance covers members, too. If you cut yourself with a prop and your own health insurance won't cover it, AMA insurance will. If a model gets away from you and causes property damage, and your homeowner's insurance doesn't cover it (many policies specifically exclude model-related accidents), your AMA insurance does. You even have a fire, theft, and vandalism rider that will allow you to recover up to $1000 of the cost of your modeling equipment if your house burns down or your car is stolen.

Does all this insurance mean that aeromodeling is unsafe? Hardly. Most of the claims that AMA handles are for minor property damage or propeller-related injuries. There are more serious accidents, but they are rare; only two fatalities related to RC aircraft have been reported to the AMA. That means there have been a lot of years of flying with no serious accidents at all. Model flying is a safe sport, and AMA members everywhere are working to keep it that way.

The AMA Safety Code

AMA insurance is governed by the Safety Code. No matter where you are, if you're involved in a modeling activity and are abiding by the Safety Code, your AMA insurance covers you. The Safety Code consists of several simple rules that really boil down to common sense—for example, don't deliberately fly over people's heads, and don't fly an untested design at a contest or large public gathering. You'll find a complete copy of the AMA Safety Code in the Appendices at the back of this book.

More Than Insurance

Insurance coverage is only one part of being an AMA member. Members receive *Model Aviation* magazine, one of the finest model magazines available. You can avail yourself of many AMA member services, from help in finding a flying site to films and videotapes. You have contest privileges at any of the more than 2000 AMA-sanctioned contests that are held each year. Your membership supports governmental liaison work that helps to keep our sport free of restrictive regulation. And of course, your membership helps to support the National Center for Aeromodeling.

The National Center is AMA's permanent home. Located near Washington, D.C., it houses AMA offices, the Lee Renaud Memorial Library, and the largest model airplane museum in the world. The Museum has been visited by thousands of tourists, Scout and school groups, and foreign visitors. AMA clubs often make special trips to the Museum, where they're met by an AMA staffer for a guided tour. Members have VIP status when they visit the

The Academy of Model Aeronautics has its headquarters in the National Center for Aeromodeling near Washington, DC. The Center houses the world's largest model airplane museum, as well as a research library and the AMA offices. (Photo courtesy AMA)

Museum; they can go through the extensive collection of model planes, look at films, or use the Renaud Library.

AMA members can be especially proud of the fact that no government grants, major foundation funding, or major corporate grants were used to build the Center. It was entirely funded by AMA members' and the model industry's contributions to the AMA Building Fund. It belongs to us all. AMA is the only aeromodeling organization in the world to have built its own permanent home.

If you're in the Washington area, be sure to come and visit the Museum. Write or call AMA for directions and hours. If you have a group, please call ahead so things will be ready for you. Groups can arrange to see the Museum during off-hours.

AMA Chartered Clubs

AMA has a network of well over 2000 chartered clubs. You can find an AMA club in every part of the country; major metropolitan areas often have several.

Joining a club is the best way in the world to enjoy aeromodeling. Most clubs have excellent flying fields where you can fly safely. Many have instructor programs that will help you build your piloting proficiency. Club meetings are a lot of fun. Most of all, there will be plenty of friendly, helpful modelers handy when you need them.

All AMA clubs require that you be an AMA member before you can use their field. This is to protect their insurance coverage. Field use is governed by the AMA Safety Code, and whatever local rules the club has put into place. Be sure that you understand these rules *and follow them*.

Get involved with your club! You can do something as simple as showing up with a rake on Spring Cleaning Day, or as complex as getting your Contest Director license and running a club meet. It doesn't matter, as long as you're involved. You'll get the most satisfaction out of your modeling that way.

The NATS

Once a year, AMA puts on the biggest model

AMA has a wide range of activities. AMA club members all over the country work to publicise aeromodeling. Here, Chip Smith explains the RC kit he's building to a visitor at the National Air and Space Museum.

meet in the world, the National Model Airplane Championships. The NATS travels around the country, being held in places like Springfield, MA; Reno, NV; Lincoln, NE; and Seguin, TX. Nowhere else will you see every single kind of model airplane flying in competition.

The NATS takes eight days, and is usually held in July or early August. Over 80 different events take place during these eight days. It takes at least three RC flying fields: one for helicopters, one for soaring, and one runway where pylon racing is flown in the morning and aerobatics in the afternoon. There has to be a paved site for the control line events, wide open spaces for free flight, and an auditorium with at least a 35-foot ceiling for indoor flying. After the official events are over, unofficial competitions pop up on the various flying sites. In the evenings there are engine collectors' get-togethers, symposia, seminars, discussion groups, exhibits, and special dinners. A free daily newspaper keeps everyone informed on all the NATS happenings.

Sometime during the week, the main RC site is opened up for a National Fun Fly. This "fly whatcha brung" event is a popular feature. You can walk up to the flight line and enjoy yourself on the same field where famous aerobatics fliers compete. Manufacturers have shown up at these, and enjoyed the chance to fly their various products.

All in all, the NATS is an experience not to be missed. Plan your vacation around one when it comes close to you. If you're an AMA member, watch *Model Aviation* for regular announcements about future NATS sites. You can call or write to AMA Headquarters for more information.

AMA members all over the country work with community groups to bring the magic of aeromodeling to people everywhere. These folks are enjoying themselves, and so are the AMA members who are helping them build Delta Dart models. (Photo by Jennifer Pratt)

MODELNET

If you have a computer and a modem to connect it to your phone, you can participate in something new in the world of model hobbies called ModelNet. ModelNet is a way to get your questions answered and find what you're looking for. It's a place to meet your friends and make new ones in a very large community. It's a list of hobby shops, model clubs, contests, and magazine articles that gets updated faster than an ordinary magazine can get printed and mailed out. It's a swap shop, a trade show, and a club meeting.

Some of all of these things are in ModelNet, and the result is something new under the sun. The beauty of it all is that this is happening all the time, and you can go there and be in it any time you want, for as long as you want, in the comfort of your own home.

ModelNet lives on CompuServe, the largest personal computer network in the USA. Compuserve is based in Columbus, Ohio. They maintain a network of local phone numbers; 80 percent of the population of the United States can reach CompuServe with a local phone call.

What Computer Do You Need? Any personal computer of any brand will work on CompuServe. The only requirements are that it must be able to connect to a modem, which connects it to the telephone, and you must have a program running on the computer that allows it to act like a terminal. Commodore 64 computers work great; so do any made by Tandy/Radio Shack. They don't have to be expensive.

What Does It Cost? Connecting to CompuServe costs you $6.25 per hour. The evening and weekend hours are when most people use the sys-

8

tem. 300 baud is the most common modem speed, and the most useful since it's just about as fast as you can read.

CompuServe has thousands of local numbers throughout the country. They can also be reached through two telephone networks, Telenet and Tymnet. You can find the numbers for your area and get more information by calling CompuServe toll-free at (800) 848-8990.

If you're one of the minority that has to dial a toll call to connect to CompuServe, you'll have to pay those charges to Ma Bell. If you are not near a city, you should check with your telephone company business office to find which CompuServe phone number will be the cheapest for you.

How Does It Work? To access CompuServe, you first subscribe to it. CompuServe subscription kits are sold at most computer stores. Some modems include a CompuServe IntroPak that allows you to sign on right away.

When you log on the first time, you will be given a number called a UserId. This is your universal ''phone number'' on the CompuServe system that serves as your identification. You will also receive a password. This keeps your CompuServe account secure, so no one else can dial up CompuServe with your UserId. You can change your password any time you choose.

When you dial CompuServe, you connect to one of their 40-odd computers, which greets you and shows you any mail you might have waiting. Then you tell CompuServe what you want to do. You can GO to an amazing number of services, from detailed weather maps that are updated every 20 minutes

Crashing? It's part of the game. Crashes all look bad right after they happen, but after you calm down, the pieces start to resemble an airplane again.

to an Electronic Mall. If you type GO MODELNET, you'll be switched into the computer where Model-Net lives.

On your first visit to ModelNet, you can look at instructions, descriptions of what's there, and information about who's running it. Then you select JOIN, and ModelNet asks for your name. You will be greeted by name whenever you log back in.

The Main Menu. The first thing you see in ModelNet is a bulletin that tells you the latest events and news. There will be a brief schedule of the next few COnferences (more on this later) and a quick description of where to find more instructions. By the way, wherever you are in CompuServe, you can always get help by simply typing ? or HELP.

Once you've read this bulletin, you won't see it again until it's updated. You can reread it and other Bulletins, though, from the Function menu.

The Function menu comes up next. It's Model-Net's "front desk," where you select what you want to do. You can read or leave messages on the

message board, go to any of the Data Libraries, go to COnference, read several Bulletins, or search the Member Directory. If you wish, you can type TOUR to see a detailed guided tour of ModelNet and how it works. Typing HELP will let you select one of several instruction files. Wherever you go, there are instructions available to help you get what you want.

The Message Board. The main area of Model-Net is the message board. It's actually 14 message boards, one for each of ModelNet's subtopics. The subtopics cover different subjects such as RC Helicopters, Plastic Models, Cars and Boats, Free Flight, Model Railroading, and the AMA NATS.

ModelNet Subtopics.

  0 General
  1 AMA Business and Contests
  2 RC Flying
  3 RC Helicopters
  4 RC Gear & Frequency Help
  5 Control Line Flying
  6 Free Flight Flying

A little epoxy, some patience mixed with stubbornness, and some help from your friends, and you're back in the air again—a little wiser than before.

7 RC Cars and Boats
8 Sport Rocketry
9 Static Models
10 Model Railroad and Railfanning
11 Computers
12 Equipment Exchange
13 The AMA NATS

When someone leaves a message on a Model-Net message board, they enter the name and UserId number of the person they want to read the message. When this person logs into ModelNet, they will be told, "You have a message waiting" and can go directly to their message. But everyone can read and respond to ModelNet messages; they are not private.

When you have read a message, you can reply to it. Suppose you read a message asking for advice about how to paint a competition model rocket. You know something about this, so you want to put in your two cents' worth. You can type RE to reply to the message. ModelNet will open a file for you to type your message into. When you're done, you type /EXIT at the beginning of a line. ModelNet then shows you a menu that allows you to continue your message, abort the message process, or store your message on the board. When you store your message, it is assigned a number and attached to the original message.

Each message has a subject. Replies to that message have the same subject. The messages, replies, and replies to the replies form a structure called a *thread*. Message threads on ModelNet form online discussions, branching out from the original message. You can look at the ModelNet messages in thread order, so you can follow the discussions and add your comments at appropriate points. At the Function menu, type RT (Read Thread) to do this.

If you want to see what messages are there, you can type BRO (browse) at the Function menu. This will show you the subject of each thread, and then ask you if you want to read that thread. If you respond Y, you are reading the thread and can RE-ply at the end of any message. If you hit return instead of typing Y, you will see the subject of the next message thread.

Suppose you have a question or comment and want to start your own discussion thread. Type L (Leave message). ModelNet will ask you who you want to leave the message to. Type the name and UserId of the person you want to read the note. The Member Directory will help you find UserIds of people you want to talk to; we'll tell you about that later. You can also type ALL for messages that you want everyone to see and answer, or type SYSOP and one of the Sysops will see it and answer.

Then ModelNet will ask you for a Subject for your message. Type in two or three words that will give people an idea of what is in your message, so they will read it.

Now ModelNet opens a file for you to type your message. Type it in, remembering that your lines should be no longer than 80 characters. You need to hit return at the end of each line. When you're done, hit return to be sure you're at the beginning of a new line, and type /EXIT. When CompuServe sees a / at the beginning of a new line, it interprets what comes after the / as a command. /EXIT takes you to the menu that lets you store your message on the ModelNet board. Type S to store it. Model-Net will ask you which subtopic you want to put your message under. Select the most relevant one. ModelNet will assign a number to your message and put it on the board where we can all see it.

The Member Directory. So how do you find other ModelNet members who share your interests? You type MD at the Function menu to access the Member Directory. The Directory lists ModelNet members by the names they entered when they joined, their UserIds, and what they're interested in. Not all ModelNet members are in this directory, since you have to make your own entry; it's not done automatically. This is to give you the opportunity to enter your interests in your MD file.

When you're making your MD entry you can list the types of models you're interested in, or anything else you'd like other ModelNet members to know about you. You can change or delete your entry at any time.

When you search the Directory, you can look for first or last names, or any part of them. You can search for UserIds to find the names of the people who own them. Most important, you can search through the interests that people have entered. Suppose you're a Control Line Stunt fanatic and looking for like-minded folks. You would search the MD for the word "stunt," and you would see the entries for everyone who had entered "stunt" in their MD listing. You can capture this list to your computer's buffer, print it out, and leave messages to these folks on the message board.

The Data Libraries. ModelNet has 15 Data Libraries, places where you can go to read files that have been uploaded by other ModelNetters. Each Data Library (DL) has a subject or specific purpose. You can see a list of the Data Libraries with the command LN (Library Names) at the Function prompt. To go to the top of any DL, type DL and the number at Function.

ModelNet Data Libraries.

0 General
1 AMA Business and Contest Calendars
2 RC Flying
3 AMA Club Index
4 Hobby Store Index
5 CL & FF Flying
6 Product Reviews Library
7 RC Cars and Boats
8 Sport Rocketry
9 Static Models
10 Model RR and Railfanning
11 Computer Programs
12 Swap Shop
13 The AMA NATS
14 Newsletter Library
15 Safety

Suppose you're looking for a hobby shop near you. Type DL 4 at Function to go to the top of DL 4, the Hobby Store Index. You see the DL menu, which gives you the opportunity to look through the files in a number of different ways. If you want a complete description of the purpose of this particular DL, you type DES at the DL menu.

The first file (usually) in each DL is a .CAT file. These Catalog files show each file in that particular DL. They are updated regularly as new files are up-

loaded. You can read these .CAT files and get the file names of the files you'd be interested in reading. Once you have the name of a file you want, you can simply type REA and the file name at the DL Menu. The file will roll up your screen; you can capture it and print it out later.

ModelNetters generally use the BRO (browse) command to look through the Data Libraries. Typing BRO shows you the files in the DL in the chronological order in which they were uploaded. It doesn't read out the whole file; it shows you the file name, the UserId of the person who uploaded the file, the length of the file, and how many times it has been read. Then you see a list of keywords and a brief description of the file written by the uploader. Finally, you see a short menu that gives you the chance to read the file, download it, or go on to the next one.

The Keywords make the BRO command more powerful. When the uploader sends his file to Model-Net, he includes a few keywords that will help you find his file. Suppose you're looking for all the files in DL 2 that have something to do with the new RC frequency plan. You use the command BRO/KEY FREQUENCY. This shows you the names and descriptions of all files that have the word FREQUENCY in their keyword lists.

COnference. The third main area of Model-Net is the conference area, usually called CO. CO is for real-time conversations. When you hit your return key, the line that you typed appears on everyone else's screen with your name in front of it in parentheses.

You get to CO by typing CO at the Function menu. There are several CO "rooms," corresponding to the message board subtopics. Everyone comes in on the same room (18), and can tune to whichever room they prefer. Multiple conversations can be going on in different rooms at the same time. You can monitor other rooms while participating in the one you're tuned to.

We have regular weekly COnferences on ModelNet, with special guests and topics for discussion. Model airplane COs are generally held on Thursday nights, and model railroad COs on Sundays. The topics are announced in the entry bulletin. CO topics are often discussed on the message board before they take place, and ModelNetters often suggest new topics for CO.

Impromptu COs are popping up all the time. While you're in ModelNet, you can see who else is logged in by typing USERS at the Function prompt or one of the DL prompts. If you spot someone you'd like to chat with, you can send them a line to invite them over to CO.

CO can be the most fun part of ModelNet once you get the hang of it. You can use it to get help with the system, find something you're looking for, or just make friends.

Who Runs ModelNet? ModelNet is one of around 200 Forums on CompuServe. It's run by the AMA as a service to all modelers. Most forums are run by a chief Sysop who is paid a commission for the connect time the Forum generates. A percentage of the connect charges that you accumulate while you're in ModelNet is donated to the AMA Museum.

I'm ModelNet's chief Sysop. Since I work at AMA headquarters, you can use ModelNet as a way of getting up-to-date information on AMA activities. Any questions about AMA business or model flying are welcome.

ModelNet also has Assistant Sysops and Subtopic Managers who answer questions and help ModelNetters in their areas of expertise. These "dial-an-experts" will quickly answer a question left under their message board subtopic. All of these folks are standing by to welcome you aboard and help you enjoy using ModelNet. We've been having fun there for over 3 years . . . come and join us!

Chapter 2

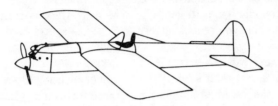

Your Workshop

THE FIRST THING YOU'RE GOING TO NEED IS A comfortable place to work. It doesn't have to be really big; during my apartment-dwelling days, I once set up my workshop in a large closet. If you want some dimensions, plan to have a table at least as long as the longest wing panel you'll be building. Six feet is quite adequate.

WORKSHOP LAYOUT

Your workshop should be well-lit. I prefer incandescent lights because I like to listen to short-wave radio as I work, and fluorescent tubes generate static. But if this isn't a problem for you, fluorescent shop fixtures are inexpensive and easy to install.

I find that overhead lighting needs to be supplemented by at least one movable lamp for close work. I have bulbs positioned over and slightly in front of my building boards, so I don't cast as much shadow over my work. The movable lamps help when I'm doing precision work on small parts, or during an electronic assembly project. I have a cou-

ple of clamp fixtures, light sockets with plastic reflectors and spring clamps on the back, that I bought at a local hardware store for about $5 each. They clamp handily onto the exposed joists in my basement workshop.

Occasionally you need light that's spotted right on your work. I found a gadget a year ago that I've come to appreciate. It's called Brighteyes, and it's a double flashlight built into a set of eyeglass-type frames. The lights are focused inward so the beams converge in front of you, and the batteries rest in containers at your temples. You can find this helpful gadget in the SIG Manufacturing catalog if your local hobby dealer doesn't have it.

Your shop should also be well-ventilated. Not that you plan to do any spray painting or any obvious gas-generating things there, but you still need good ventilation. Some of the glues we use give off fumes. There are other chemicals in common modeling materials that you can wind up breathing. Even iron-on coverings give off fumes as you iron them down. Then there's balsa dust, to which some of us are allergic. So provide yourself with a window or some other source of adequate ventilation.

ADHESIVES

You're going to need glue. Furthermore, you're going to need several different glues. Different tasks require different types of adhesives. There's a bewildering array of glues available in your hobby store.

Back in the 1930s, people dissovled old toothbrush handles in acetone to make model airplane cement. Movie film also worked well. I can remember using those tricks, although I'm not that old; I lived in a small town, and I depended on the U.S. Mail for my hobby supplies.

You're unlikely to find one glue that suits all your purposes, although several come close. The best bet is to have several different kinds handy so you have some when you need it. Then buy large bottles of the glue you prefer.

Cyanoacrylate Glues

In the past five years, glue technology has revolutionized the way we build model airplanes. The so-called "super glues" are *alpha-cyanoacrylates,* compounds that form long chain molecules when chemically catalyzed. They "dry" through a chemical reaction, rather than by the evaporation of a solvent. That's why you hear references to CyA glues "going off" or "activating" instead of "drying."

Incidentally, there is no real generic term for these glues. "Super Glue" is a trade name, as is "Krazy Glue" and even "CA." The leaders in the field wound up with the same problem as Kleenex and Aspirin: Their trade names became used as generics. Hot Stuff, Jet, and Zap are both nouns and verbs in common usage, and you'll hear people talking about "Zapping" a plane back together or "Jetting" a fuselage. The confusing thing is, they could have been using Hot Stuff!

After wrestling with the problems for a while, most of the magazines started using the term "CyA" to refer to all cyanoacrylate glues. Unless I'm referring to a specific brand, that's the term I'll use.

CyA Glue Safety. There are some safety problems that you should be aware of when using super glues. First and foremost, they will bond skin almost instantly. This is seldom more than an annoyance, since the oil in the surface of your skin quickly releases the bond. But don't panic and try to pull away quickly when you find yourself glued to the piece you're working on! Take your time, apply one of the debonders, and work it loose slowly. You will be free in about 30 seconds, with all your original skin intact.

Second, you should remember that the setting of CyA glue is a chemical process. In the course of going off, all CyA glues give off heat and gas. The heat is noticeable when a drop of CyA glue on your hand that you didn't notice goes off. The fumes are a strong eye irritant. Don't get too close to your work, or you'll catch this puff of irritating gas right in the face.

If you do, don't panic. CyA fumes are an irritant, nothing more. Stand up and move to another area for a few moments. It goes away quickly, leaving you with a lesson well-learned. That's the main reason why your workshop should be well-ventilated!

Finally, some people are allergic to CyA glues. This might not show up right away. I've known people who have built up an allergy over a period of years, to the point where now they can't bear to be around the stuff. If you think this could be happening to you, see a doctor and take a bottle of the suspect glue along. Allergies like these are rare, but they do exist, so caution is advised.

Grades of CyA Glues. When they were originally introduced, CyA glues were of limited usefulness, since they required a perfect fit between the glued parts. Now there are different grades available that will fill gaps between poorly fitting parts. Accelerators are sold that set the super glues instantly. And debonding agents are available that will separate a CyA glue joint with no damage to the glued pieces.

Thin CyA glue (Hot Stuff, Instant Jet, Regular Zap, Pic Stic, etc.) soaks quickly into porous surfaces. It requires a perfect fit between the surfaces to be glued. But it is the most "instant" of the CyA glues. Dripped into the crack between two wood pieces, it goes off within 15 seconds, forming a bond that is stronger than the original material.

Medium grade CyA (Hot Stuff Super T, Regular Jet, Regular Zap, etc.) is the most all-around useful of the CyA glues. I buy the stuff in the largest bottles I can find. Since it fills small gaps, parts fit doesn't have to be perfect. It doesn't soak into the pieces as quickly as the thin CyAs, so it can be used on very porous surfaces such as the edges of balsa sheets. And it takes about 30 seconds to a minute to go off, giving you time to reposition the pieces if necessary.

Another nice thing about medium grades of CyA is that they will usually bond oily surfaces. They're great for repairs in the engine compartment, for example.

Thick CyA (Slow Jet, Slo-Zap, etc.) is stronger than the thinner grades, and will fill fair-sized holes. It can take as long as two minutes to go off, making it ideal for parts that have to be positioned, such as wing sheeting or long leading edge strips.

There are other specialized CyA glues on the market as well. Flex Zap is a super-strong grade of thick CyA, with the highest shear strength I've seen. I use it in places where I usually use epoxy, such as around the firewall in the engine compartment. I've also discovered that Flex Zap is resistant to the usual debonders, so don't use it casually; if there's a chance that the piece will have to be reglued, use another grade. You can always run Flex Zap over the glue joint after you're certain.

A company called Penn Industrial Chemicals has brought out a line of glues called Pic Stic. It's available in the three common grades. There's also a Pic Stic just for gluing plastic, and several grades of epoxy as well as other useful chemicals.

For more on how to work with CyA glues, see Chapter 5 on covering and finishing. That's where we examine how to sand off the excess glue that hardens out on the surface, among other things.

CyA Accelerators. There are several products that allow you to chemically set CyA glues. They work at different speeds and with different effects, but they are all similar; you spray them on and the glue "goes off." Accelerators make life so much easier, that they've become standard equipment in most modelers' workshops.

Satellite City, makers of Hot Stuff, have an accelerator called Hot Shot. Pacer, the Zap people, have an accelerator called Zip Kicker. PIC produces an accelerator called PIC Pronto. All of these come in pushbutton-type applicators. They set off the glue very quickly; thin CyA will set so rapidly it'll crackle.

Goldberg, producers of Jet CyA, has an accelerator called Jet Set. It comes in a pressurized spray can. Jet Set lays down a thinner shot of accelerator over a wider area than the pushbutton applicators. It doesn't set the glue off as fast as the other products, which is useful for places where you need a few seconds to position the parts.

One of the most useful tricks for using accelerators is pre-spraying one side. Suppose you need a really strong joint, or you have two rough surfaces that don't make perfect contact. Give one surface a shot of accelerator. Apply CyA glue to the other side, and mate the pieces. The glue will go off quickly and form a very solid joint. You should use the thicker grades of CyA for this, since thin CyA will soak into the surface very quickly. Jet Set's tendency to accelerate curing more slowly than the other products makes it useful for this trick.

All of the CyA accelerators will evaporate rapidly if they're left uncapped. They have a high vapor pressure and will fizzle out of the pushbutton applicators under their own pressure. They also have the characteristic of gradually eroding the plastic nozzles of any of the applicators I've used. This means that toward the bottom of the bottle, you're likely to get larger and larger drops of accelerator sprayed on your work surface. This is why I don't buy the largest bottles of accelerator; I've tried refilling them, but the applicators are pretty much useless after the second or third refill. I'm still looking for a really good applicator for this stuff, but until some enterprising company comes out with one, what we've got works okay.

CyA Storage. CyA glues have a definite shelf life, usually a year or less. They are extremely hygroscopic, which means that they attract moisture out of the atmosphere. After the bottle is opened and air is allowed inside, they will gradually thicken and turn yellow. For this reason, it's best to keep your glue bottles capped when they're not actually in use. CyA glues are packaged in a nitrogen atmosphere so they will be moisture-free until opened.

You can extend the shelf life of CyA almost indefinitely by storing the bottles in a plastic bag in your refrigerator. When you take them out, be certain to allow them to come up to room temperature before you open the bottles. The cold will condense moisture onto the bottles, and if you open them you know where that moisture will go and what it'll do! Don't be afraid to stock up on CyA if the local hobby shop has a sale, but be aware of the limited shelf life. This is why I prefer to get my glue at a local store where I know what they have is fresh.

Aliphatic Resin Glues

Woodworkers frequently use a type of glue called *aliphatic resin*. The most popular brand is Franklin's Titebond, but there are several others available in hobby stores. They are recognizable by their brownish color. Aliphatic resin glues are water-based, so these can be thinned and cleaned off your fingers with water.

They are very useful for wood, because they soak into the grain of the wood and provide a bond that is usually stronger than the surrounding wood. I have a bottle of aliphatic resin glue handy for places where I don't want the quick grab of a CyA glue—for example, when sliding one piece into a slot or hole in another. CyA glue will go off quickly when it is spread into a thin film by sliding two parts together. Using a resin glue will give just as strong a joint, and it won't freeze up on you before you have the pieces positioned where you want them!

Resin glues fill gaps between mating surfaces much better than most grades of CyA glue. Since it takes longer to set, it will soak more deeply into harder woods than will a CyA glue. Consider using it for engine mounting rails, servo mounts, or other places where you have to glue a hardwood like maple, mahogany, or basswood.

Many builders prefer to use aliphatic resin glue for sheeting a fuselage or wing with thin balsa sheets. The reason for this is that most wing sheeting has to be butt-joined along the edges to cover the wing, and it's well-nigh impossible to do this without excess glue oozing up through the joint and drying on the surface. Aliphatic resin glue sands very easily, and is near the hardness of the surrounding wood. This means that when you smooth off the sheeted surface with a sanding block, you will be able to sand right down to the surface of the joint, removing the ridge of glue.

Casein Glues

Casein (or white) glues are probably the most common household glues. They're made from milk, and are completely nontoxic and perfectly safe for small children. For this reason, if you're helping your daughter or son put together their first balsa wood model airplane, you should probably let them use casein glue rather than a CyA. It also washes easily out of their clothes.

Casein glues are easily recognized by their white color. The most common brand is Elmer's Glue, familiar to every schoolchild. I must have used gallons of this stuff when I was a child, building rockets, hand-launched gliders, and free-flight jobs. It's just as useful today. Its major virtues are similar to the aliphatic resins: gap-filling ability, great penetration, and good strength. You can easily use casein glues to form fillets. Thinned 50/50 with water and brushed onto exposed balsa, it makes a good quick grain filler and sealer. Its sanding qualities are excellent, like the aliphatic resin glues mentioned above.

White glues are not as strong as aliphatic resins, and they are not waterproof when they are dry. They also shrink as they dry, so fillets should be allowed to dry completely (at least 24 hours) before being painted over. I've found that out the hard way once or twice, when the glue shrank away from the hardened paint leaving a thin bubble of paint where the fillet was supposed to be.

Epoxy

Epoxy glues have a lot of use in model construction. They're fuelproof, easy to use, and very

Epoxy glues are available with several different working times. The most useful are the five-minute epoxies, for fast repairs, and the 30-minute epoxies for construction and finishing. 30-minute epoxy penetrates the wood better, causing a tighter bond. (Photo courtesy *Model Aviation* magazine)

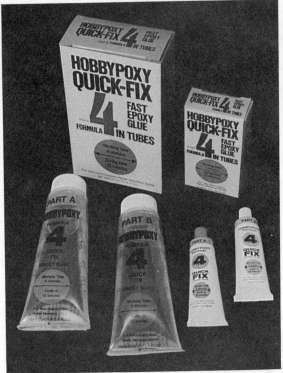

Epoxies are widely used to glue dissimilar materials, to fuel-proof engine compartments, and for repairs, especially on plastic foam. Hobbypoxy Formula 4 sets up in four minutes for fast repairs. (Photo courtesy *Model Retailer* magazine)

strong. They bond everything, as long as the surfaces are clean and oil-free.

There's a brand of epoxy made specifically for hobby use, called HobbyPoxy. It's available in different grades, determined by the curing time. I get the most use out of Formula 4, which has a working time of four or five minutes. This is perfect for joining wings, reinforcing landing gear mounts, and installing firewalls.

Hobbypoxy also has an epoxy glue that is thixotropic. This means that it has the consistency of a gel unless you're actually working it. You scoop equal parts of the thixotropic epoxy out of the cans and mix. Under pressure, the two parts flow together like a liquid. When you apply this glue it stays right where you put it, without running. It can be

very useful for things such as installing servo rails or wing dowels.

Plastic Glues

Occasionally you have to work with plastic in the process of building RC models. This is usually in the form of engine cowls, wheel pants, and windshields. For these parts, you'll need a plastic glue.

I shy away from the tube-type styrene cements for these parts. They're specifically formulated for plastic models, and are seldom suitable for the plastics we use. Liquid plastic cement works much better. Put the pieces together and flow the liquid cement into the joint.

There are a few CyA type glues that are formulated for plastics. Pacer's Plasti Zap and PIC's

Plastic Stic are the most common. These work very well on RC model plastic parts, and have the other virtues of CyA glues. Accelerators will set them off, too.

Clear windshields are a special case. Many glues will fog the plastic as they set. Some CyA accelerators will fog them, too. I prefer to use a glue called RC-56, made by Wilhold, for clear plastics. It dries clear, doesn't fog, and sticks all kinds of plastics. Working it is a lot like using white glue. You can put masking tape over it to hold the windshield or canopy in place. It takes a few hours to dry, and once it's dried it can be trimmed and sanded. It will stick to plastic coverings. Most hobby stores carry RC-56 just for use on clear plastics.

FILLERS

Nothing is perfect, and you're going to find a lot of places where you want to fix imperfections. A good filler material is the answer. It can help you make joints disappear, fill in dings and dents, and even do minor repairs. It can help you form fillets and reinforcing joints between surfaces. The right filler will make your life a lot easier.

I use two fillers for different applications: Model Magic and Sig Epoxolite. They're very different products with different virtues.

Model Magic has become the standard filler compound used for RC models. It resembles spackling compound; it's white, comes in a plastic tub, and thins with water. But it costs more than spackling, and there are some very good reasons. Model Magic has a better adhesion to wood and plastic than any other filler I've used. It doesn't attack any of the common materials we use, so you can use it for patching foam wings or forming fillets around the edge of a clear plastic canopy. It has the same hardness as balsa wood, so it sands right down to the wood without leaving ridges. It dries quickly, usually within 15 minutes.

I have developed a few techniques for working with Model Magic. I use a palette knife to apply fillers and epoxies. It has a very flexible blade, and it's perfect for working the stuff into small cracks. I bought the palette knife at an art supply store, but a lot of hobby shops carry them in their brush display.

It takes very little water to thin Model Magic. You don't want to thin it too much, unless you're using it as a grain filler prior to painting. I use the palette knife to work up a pocket of filler in the tub. A single drop of water will let you whip the Model Magic like meringue. Fluff it up and it'll spread easier and work into smaller cracks.

The other filler I use extensively, Epoxolite, is very different. Epoxolite's main virtue is its strength. This stuff is strong enough to bear structural loads. You can form fillets from it or use it to reinforce load-bearing areas. It will fill in the space between landing gear wires to make fairings. If you're building a scale model and the wheel pant fairs into the strut, Epoxolite will not only form the fairing but will securely hold the wheel pant in place. When it sets it can be drilled, filed, and sanded.

Epoxolite is mixed from equal parts of resin and hardener. It's easy to do, since the parts are of different colors. Its a good idea to get it as smooth as you can when you apply it; it sets up pretty hard, and since it usually goes into hard-to-reach areas, sanding can be difficult. Epoxolite smooths very nicely with a wet finger.

You can get Epoxolite, as well as all other SIG products, from your local hobby shop. If you don't have a hobby shop, by all means write for the SIG catalog. It's a valuable reference book in itself.

BUILDING BOARDS

Your building board is one of your most essential pieces of equipment. You really can't do much without one. If the building surface you use isn't straight and true, your planes won't fly right (and may not fly at all).

You want an absolutely flat surface, at least three feet long and two feet wide. This should be large enough to build any average wing panel or fuselage side you'll encounter right away. Of course, the larger the plane, the larger the building board you'll need. On the advice of my old friend Bob Hoeckele, once editor of *Flying Models* magazine, I acquired a solid wooden door. You can often find doors at hardware stores that have some sort of defect that makes them unusable as doors, like a scratch or knot. I've even seen doors with the hole for the knob drilled at the wrong spot. You should be able to buy the door cheaply, and give it a new purpose in life as an ideal building board.

The board needs some sort of surface that you can stick pins into to hold parts in place as you work on them. I use large, flat acoustical ceiling tiles, which cost a couple of bucks apiece. I use wood screws in the corners to hold the tile flat against my building board. When they get scarred up from use, you toss 'em out and screw down new ones.

The ceiling tile accepts pins beautifully. It also makes an excellent cutting surface, since it won't dull a thin blade that cuts all the way through the piece you're working on. I use map tacks to hold plans on the board, and T-pins to secure the parts over the plan.

Some folks use cork for a building surface, but it's awfully expensive and not always perfectly smooth. Wallboard such as Homasote will work well, and is available in larger pieces than acoustical tile. Pick out a piece with as smooth a surface as possible.

Peck-Polymers sells building boards in two different sizes, 12 by 18 and 18 by 24 inches. These are made from hard balsa, and are surfaced absolutely smooth. For $7 and $8 respectively, they're a bargain. If you build small models, you should have one of these.

TOOLS AND ACCESSORIES

There is an unbelievable array of tools and accessories available for the RC modeler. No matter what you want to do, someone has produced something to make it easier for you to do it. Many of these come from very small companies, often just one man producing the device in his garage or basement. The products are often of a very high quality since they're made by hand. The disadvantage is that these small firms often don't have the distribution or marketing resources necessary to make their products easily available. It makes the job of the hobby dealer more interesting, tracking down and stocking literally dozens of things that his customers

ask for that aren't available through normal distribution channels.

I'm not going to be able to list all of the accessories you can buy, but I'll cover the ones I know of. We'll look at building accessories here, and flying accessories in Chapter 6.

The key to a good-looking model is sanding. How much you sanded the model is a direct measure of how successful it's going to be, so any tool that makes sanding easier is very desirable. ADC Tee-Bars are long t-shaped extrusions of aluminum with sandpaper glued to the flat side. They make it very easy to sand long surfaces, such as fuselage sides or wing leading edges, perfectly straight. I also use several Perma Grit tools, which have metal abrasives permanently adhered to a series of different shapes. The flexible steel Perma Grits are most useful during construction.

You can't get along without sanding blocks. There are many available at hardware and paint stores, but I haven't found one better than the Wedge Lock. Wedge Lock blocks use a sanding belt rather than gripping a strip of sandpaper at both ends like most blocks. It takes seconds to swap belts for different grits or move the belt to a less worn spot. Ace RC makes several sanding tools that have grit deposited on different diameters of dowel. The pointed ones are especially useful. Finally, I have a tiny one-inch wide sanding block made by Applied Design and sold in hobby shops. It has a strip of sandpaper wrapped around a thick layer of foam, making it quite flexible. It gets inside fuselages and into tight corners.

For knives, I use the faithful old X-Acto number 11. I keep lots of blades handy, though; they dull quickly. Two sizes of razor saws are very useful. These thin bladed saws have very fine teeth and are perfect for cutting through balsa blocks or spruce. For detail or precision work I favor the Uber Sciver knife, sold by *Model Builder* magazine. These are just as sharp as a razor blade and much easier to work with. Their only drawback is that the thin blades are fragile and can snap if you use them for harder work than they are intended.

I have an assortment of different files that come in handy. They don't have to be too expensive, since

This support is an Ace Super Cradle. The handle moves along the base for balance, and the supports in the front hold the wing on the way to the field.

balsa wood won't give them much resistance. A set of Allen wrenches and screwdrivers of different sizes are essential. Try to get at least a few screwdrivers with very long blades, so you can reach past engines to tighten motor mount screws.

A small hand drill is another essential item. Cordless rechargeable types will work beautifully for model building. There are lots of places where you need a gentle, precise touch; for these I use the Ace Handrills set. The Handrills are shaped wooden grips with drill bits fitted. They're very sharp and will do a lot of jobs. Finally, Harry Higley sells several sizes of drill bits that have shanks over two feet long. These are perfect for drilling holes deep inside fuselages, which you will find you need to do from time to time when installing pushrods—especially the throttle pushrod.

Every now and then you run out of hands, and need to hold something in place while working on it. Small cloth bags filled with sand or lead shot are just what's needed for this. Bell Rock Industries sells a set of bags called "Weight Mates" that do the job nicely and are very inexpensive. Your hobby shop will have them.

Chapter 3

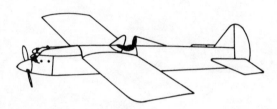

What You Need to Know about Radio Systems

THIS CHAPTER WILL TELL YOU BASIC INFORMATION about radio control systems. If you're a beginner, read this chapter before you buy your first radio. We'll explain a lot of the terms you will hear experts use when they describe a radio, and discuss how important they are.

If you're not a beginner, you'll find useful information here on the new RC frequency allotment scheme that is in place. Major changes are happening in 1988 and 1991. This chapter will give you an idea of how this affects you.

WHERE IT ALL CAME FROM

When RC began, you had to be an amateur radio operator to run the transmitter. This meant passing a test (and learning Morse code) to get the license, and paying a fee. It also meant building your own radio system, usually from scratch. The pioneers of RC, like Walt and Bill Good, combined modeling with their experience in ham radio because there was no other way.

As RC grew and matured, people began looking for ways to make it easier to get involved. AMA was instrumental in getting a portion of the radio spectrum (a *band*) set aside for radio control use. Eventually the license became a formality: Send in the application and get the ticket. A few years ago the license requirement was dropped completely.

THE FREQUENCY PHASE-IN PLAN

RC experienced rapid growth in the 1970s and '80s. AMA responded by working with the Federal Communications Commission to ease the restrictions and accommodate the growth. In 1981 a band of 80 new frequencies was granted for radio control use, 50 for aircraft and 30 for surface models.

AMA has been managing the transition by establishing a Phase-in Plan. This plan is intended to make sure that modelers could use their existing equipment for as long as possible, while encouraging them to have their radio systems retuned to the new frequencies, or to buy modern equipment.

Before 1981 we had seven frequencies in the 72 MHz band. They were designated by two-color codes: 72.160 was blue and white, for example. Fliers hung ribbons of these colors from their transmitter antennas so people could tell what frequency they were transmitting on. The frequencies were widely separated, so the receivers didn't have to be too selective.

In 1981, 11 new frequencies opened up. They're designated by channel numbers: 12, 38, 40, 42, up to 56. The area between Channel 12 and 36 is occupied by five of the old frequencies. Note that these new channels are all even numbers. That's to maintain a spacing of 40 kilohertz (kHz) between channels, which is safe for the old receivers still in use.

In 1988 the old frequencies disappear, and even-numbered slots between 12 and 38 open. At this point, everyone has to have either a new radio system, or an old one retuned to one of the new frequencies.

In 1991 the odd-numbered channels open up. At this point, you should have a receiver that's capable of operating at a channel spacing of 20 kHz instead of 40. When you see an ad that describes a radio as a "1991 system," it should mean that the receiver is capable of operating safely with other transmitters on either side of it, 20 kHz away from its frequency.

AMA'S TRANSMITTER TESTING PROGRAM

Since early 1986, AMA has been checking transmitters at trade shows. They use a spectrum analyzer, a bulky and expensive piece of equipment that displays radio energy on a screen. Switch on your transmitter, and the spectrum analyzer shows how much energy it's broadcasting, and precisely where that energy is.

When they test your transmitter, they look to be sure that it is putting out most of its energy on your assigned channel. If it's off a little, no problem, but you should be aware of it. If it's off a *lot*, it could cause interference to the channel next to you.

The next thing they look for is how much energy your transmitter is producing on either side of its designated frequency. The energy your transmitter produces is displayed as a steep curve or spike. The sides of this spike spread out and down. If they spread too far out too close to the top of the spike, they can cause interference to neighboring channels. The standard they're looking for is 20 dB down at 50 kHz out. This means that the sides of the spike need to be 20 decibels down from the peak at 25 kilohertz away from the peak to either side. Again, if your transmitter doesn't quite measure up, you can get advice on how to have it properly tuned. Most of the transmitters sold today are easily tunable by a technician with the proper equipment.

Incidentally, this is a good reason not to settle for the cheapest radio system you can find: The better the system, the easier it'll be to keep it properly tuned.

THE STRAIGHT WORD ON INTERFERENCE

Any radio you buy should be on a new frequency. It's easy to tell; if the frequency is a numbered channel, it's one of the new ones. Your hobby dealer might have some advice on which frequency to buy, based on his customers' experience. In some parts of the country, some frequencies are subject to interference from commercial broadcasters that are between our channels and are splashing on us. Legally, our channels are ours alone, and no one should be causing us interference. But practically, there are so many TV and radio stations, paging services, industrial radio systems, and so on that you can't expect the FCC to inspect them all and keep them right where they belong. With the relatively large number of RC channels available, there will certainly be plenty of "clean" ones wherever you care to fly.

If you or your fellow fliers are experiencing what you think could be interference problems, AMA has a program to help you. A District Frequency Coordinator has been appointed for your area. His job is to keep track of interference problems. He needs to know about problems you experience; if he's getting similar reports from your area, he'll investigate. You'll find a list of District Frequency Coordinators in Appendix G of this book; contact the one closest to you or AMA Headquarters if you have more questions.

HOW MUCH DO YOU HAVE TO SPEND?

Do you really need an expensive radio system? That depends. If you're going to fly in the middle of nowhere, with no other fliers around who will have their radios turned on while you're in the air, you can probably get away with something cheap. But think twice before you go for the cheapest radio on the dealer's shelf or in the catalog. If it doesn't do what you need, it's no bargain. A poor radio is worse; it could wind up costing you an airplane.

Some fliers prefer a single-stick transmitter. This puts rudder, aileron, and elevator on the same stick; the rudder is moved by turning the stick assembly. Throttle is on the left stick. Here, Doug Christensen is using a Multiplex radio system.

There is a very wide variety of radios to choose from. You can narrow down your choice by focusing on your needs. You will almost certainly need four or more channels: one each for elevator, aileron, throttle and rudder. Even if you have a sailplane, or a small .049-powered job with only rudder and elevator, I recommend a four-channel system. Sooner or later, you'll need all the channels.

What about the under-$60 two-channel radio systems? Well, they're really best for RC cars and boats. I'm not saying that you can't fly a two-channel airplane with a two-channel twin stick radio, but it's not easy. Having rudder on the right stick is natural enough, since you'd use that thumb to turn the plane with a conventional setup. But using your left thumb for elevator will throw you a curve when you try to fly something that puts both these functions on a single stick. You'll have a lot of reflexes to unlearn before you can make the transition. So leave the two-channel twin stick systems for the surface models, where it's perfectly natural to use the left stick for forward and reverse.

Cox Hobbies used to produce a three-channel system with rudder and elevator on a single two-axis stick, and a slide switch on the left for throttle. I really liked this system and was sorry to see it go. However, at a recent trade show, they showed me a prototype of a new three-channel single stick system, so it should be available in stores by the time you read this. Kraft Systems produced a similar system for about a year before they ceased operations. It, too, was excellent for small models and sailplanes. You will occasionally see systems like this in catalogs, but they are often priced so that you might as well buy a four-channel system anyway.

More Than Four Channels? What do we need with more than four channels? The fifth channel is usually a simple switch. The servo is all the way at one end of its travel, and throwing the switch moves it all the way over the other way. This is intended to operate retractable landing gear, but can also be used to switch a function on and off. For example, a sailplane can use this function for a releasable towhook. With a simple electronic switch, such as the unit sold by RAM Inc. or McDaniel RC, you can turn a lighting system on and off.

Seven channel systems incorporate this fifth switched channel, plus two more proportional channels. These are operated by slide switches or knobs. I've used these extra channels for flaps, spoilers, and lighting systems where moving the switch different distances turns different sets of lights on or off. Advanced Pattern (aerobatics) airplanes sometimes use these extra functions for in-flight adjustment of the needle valve on the engine, or for variable-pitch props.

Radio System Prices. You should be able to buy a good four-channel radio for around $200. Your hobby shop will occasionally have specials as low as $150. A five, six or seven-channel system will cost between $200 and $600.

This cost includes rechargeable nickel-cadmium (ni-cad) batteries in the transmitter, and in a separate smaller pack for the receiver. You'll also get a charger that will charge these packs at the overnight rate.

The system will also include servos, usually four, even with the systems that have more than four channels. The servos you need for the extra functions should cost between $20 and $50 apiece, unless you need something special.

Some mail-order catalogs will list radios for less than you can buy them in your hobby store. Should you buy mail order? If you know what you're doing, you'll probably be okay. But frankly, I prefer to have the store nearby when I need service, parts, or advice. That's why I pay the extra $20 or so and buy it at the hobby shop.

What's Good and What Isn't? Almost everything that you can buy today is good. All modern radio systems are far more reliable than they were a few years ago. For that reason, you're better off buying a new, modern system than a used one. A used radio might be tuned to an old frequency that you'd have to get changed. You don't know how well it's been maintained or what kind of use it's been through. And it might be hard to get parts for it.

There are some radio systems that cost less than $200 for a four-channel set. Polk's Model Craft Hobbies imports a system that is very inexpensive. It doesn't include rechargeable batteries, so you'll have to buy battery cells and a charger.

Futaba makes the meat-and-potatoes radio systems that you'll find at most club fields. The popularity of Futaba systems is an advantage, because parts are widely available.

The ACOMS radios imported through Altech Marketing and sold in hobby stores are very competitively priced. I have used three ACOMS systems for years and am very pleased with them. The receivers have proven to be very good at rejecting adjacent channel interference and intermodulation. (We'll discuss interference in detail later in this chapter.)

Airtronics imports an excellent line of radio systems, recognizable by their brushed aluminum transmitter cases. I have used several Airtronics radios for years and never had a problem with them. Parts availability is also excellent.

Ace RC radios are a bit unusual. Designed and made in America, they are sometimes more expensive than imported radios with similar features. But they have a reputation for excellent reliability. Ace makes an inexpensive basic radio, the Olympic 5, that comes with ni-cad batteries but without servos. Their Silver Seven radio has a very good reputation among experts for rejecting interference. Silver Seven radios are available as kits, so you can save money and end up with a very good radio if you have some experience assembling electronic devices. You

Airtronics imports the excellent Sanwa radios; they are available with a wide range of features. (Photo courtesy Airtronics, Inc.)

can even customize the transmitter, putting all the switches and controls right where you want them.

JR radios are imported by Circus Hobbies in Las Vegas. They are available in some hobby stores. I have used two JR Century VII seven-channel systems for some time with very good results. They have a wide assortment of useful features.

World Engines imports a series of radios at a very low price. I haven't used any of their systems, but I know that they are in wide use.

Several other brands are imported into the U.S., such as Multiplex and Simprop. These are full-featured, expensive expert systems.

RADIO SYSTEM CARE

Your radio system is just like your stereo or VCR: It requires care in handling. A radio control system is designed to take abuse in the course of its use, but it'll work much better if you don't abuse it!

When you install your receiver in the plane, wrap it in foam rubber. Vibration is one of the chief killers of electronic equipment, and even the smoothest-running engines vibrate. Those vibrations are transmitted through the fuselage. If you just use double-sided foam tape to secure your receiver, it's going to get full benefit of all that shaking. Use real foam rubber, not the stuff that sometimes comes in packing crates. That foam is intended to cushion against shocks rather than vibration, and can transmit engine vibration right through to the receiver.

Your transmitter is a precision instrument; treat it as such. Don't put it on the floor of your car or in the trunk to get bounced around on the way to the field. Don't leave it on a car seat in direct sunlight. If you drop it, range-check your system. A little extra care with your tranny can save an airplane!

Lots of expert pilots buy special cases for their transmitters. These are similar to camera cases, and protect the transmitter in shock-resistant foam. Not only is the transmitter safe from accidents, but the trim switches don't get moved by accident either.

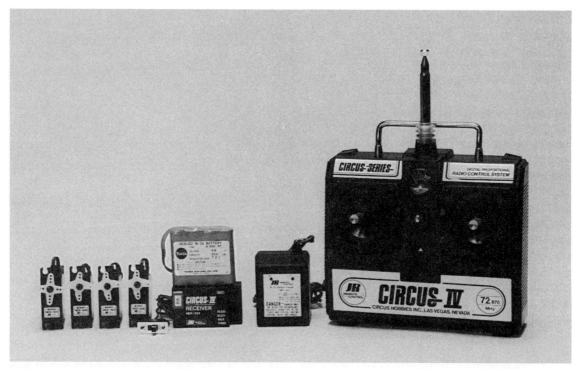

JR Radios are imported by Circus Hobbies in Las Vegas. This is the Circus 4, an inexpensive basic radio system. (Photo courtesy *Model Retailer* magazine)

This helps prevent unpleasant surprises right after takeoff.

BATTERIES

You will spend more time charging and caring for your batteries than any other regular maintenance task. There are very good reasons for this. *Flying Models* magazine did a survey several years ago that asked readers about the major causes of crashed airplanes. Way out in first place was improperly charged batteries. More people lost their favorite airplanes because they forgot to charge the night before, or figured that they could get one more flight without recharging their receiver pack.

Balancing Your Battery Packs. When your radio system is new and the batteries are flat, they should be charged for 24 hours before use. This gives the new packs a full charge to start out with, and also balances the pack. *Balancing* refers to the fact that ni-cad cells will accept and release their charge at slightly different rates. So as the pack is charged or used, each cell will have a little more or less charge in it than the other cells in the pack.

As the pack approaches full discharge, it can happen that one of the cells will reach the end of its charge before the others. The other cells will be pouring current through the flat cell, and this current will "charge" the cell in reverse. This can ruin the cell in short order. As a battery pack gets older, cell reversal becomes more and more likely. When a pack finally quits, you will often find that several of the cells are reversed, showing a negative voltage when you touch a voltmeter leads to the cell's terminals.

The best way to prevent cell reversal is to slow-charge the batteries with the charger that came with the radio, and be sure that you give them enough time on the charger.

Cell Memory. Ni-cad cells are also subject to a condition called *memory*. Memory can happen when you fully charge your pack before each use and discharge it to about the same point each time you use it. Do this often enough and the cell might quit producing current at that point, even though there is capacity remaining. If one cell in the pack does

this, you'll notice a sharp reduction in the capacity of the pack.

Memory can be avoided by cycling your packs regularly. This means discharging them to a safe level and slow-charging them to full charge again. There are other good reasons for battery cycling; we'll discuss them later in this chapter.

Charge Speeds and Currents. Ni-cad batteries can accept a charge at different rates. This rate, measured in milliamps ($\frac{1}{1000}$ of an amp) is determined by the capacity of the cells, measured in milliamp/hours. Most of the batteries we use in radio control systems are 500 or 550 milliamp/hour cells. This means that they will supply a current of 500 milliamps steadily for an hour, or 1 amp (1000 milliamps) for ½ hour, or 250 milliamps for two hours, etc. The abbreviation for milliamps is mA, and for milliamp/hours is mAh.

Charge current is measured in amps. Charge rates are usually described as a fraction of cell capacity. C is the abbreviation for cell capacity. Therefore, a charge rate of C/10 would indicate a current of $\frac{1}{10}$ the mAh rating of the cell. For 500 mAh cells, the C/10 charge rate is 50 mA. For 1200 mAh cells (sub-C size), the C/10 rate is 120 mA. Simple, huh?

C/10 is the charge rate you'll get out of the charger that comes with the radio. It safely charges the batteries to full capacity in 16 hours. The batteries can stand considerable overcharge at this rate too, since there isn't enough current flowing through them to generate heat. This is why chargers that charge faster are seldom sold with the radio system; C/10 may not be fast, but it won't destroy battery packs.

Sometimes we need to charge at other rates than C/10. There are four standard charge rates: trickle charge, regular charge, quick charge, and fast charge. Regular charge is the C/10 rate we've been discussing.

Trickle charging is charging at the rate of C/100. This is a very low charge current, and hardly actually charges the cells at all. But it's useful for battery packs that are already fully charged. This is because all ni-cad cells will lose their charge all by themselves if left alone. This self-discharging means that you had better not charge your batteries one weekend, and go flying the next weekend without giving them a few more hours on the charger!

Trickle charging at the C/100 rate puts just enough charge back into the cells to compensate for their natural tendency to self-discharge. You can bring a pack up to full charge, and then put it on a trickle charge to keep it peaked for a long period of time—weeks, if necessary.

Ace RC sells a charger that does just this. It's called the Charge Master, and it can charge two transmitter batteries and four receiver batteries at once. Once each pack is at full charge, you can switch the output for that pack over to trickle charge. The Charge Master was made for the weekend flier who wants to keep his planes ready to go, and it really does the job. It's also a very good kit to learn electronic assembly with.

Quick charging is charging at the C rate. In other words, you're putting the same amperage into the cells that you will get out. To quick charge a 500 mAh pack, you would charge it at 500 mA. This will bring the pack up to full charge in around three hours.

Fast charging is done at a rate of 3C, three times the rated capacity of the cells. Before trying a fast charge, you should be certain that your cells can handle it! Many smaller cells supplied with radio systems can't take the current of a fast charge. On the other hand, most batteries larger than 550 mAh capacity can handle fast charge current.

To fast charge a 500 mAh battery pack, you would set your charger at a current of 1500 mAh, or 1.5 amps. This should fully charge the pack in about 20 minutes. To charge a pack of 1200 mAh cells in 20 minutes, you would need to charge at a current of 3600 mAh, or 3.6 amps. This is what fast-chargers for RC car battery packs do.

Field Fast Charging. Your radio system batteries will seldom be set up for 3C charging. It really isn't necessary. Say you've been out flying all day, and have about two hours of on-time on your system. You check the receiver pack with an ESV, and decide that it's time to charge them. You can quit

for the day and put them on the charger at home, or you can *field charge* them.

To field charge, you need a system that will put a higher charge rate than the normal into your transmitter and receiver packs. There are several chargers on the market that will do this. A Leisure Electronics Digital Charger will put a charge in packs of from four to eight cells, of any capacity. An Astro Flight charger will do the job too. The Robbe Automax 8 will charge transmitter and receiver packs, and do it automatically through a three-stage charge cycle.

There are several important things to be aware of if you are using a fast charger to field charge your system. Never use a charger that doesn't allow you to set the charge current. A constant-current charger such as the ones listed above will not put more amps into your battery pack than you set it for. Too much amperage and you risk overheating and venting a cell. And with that receiver pack buried in the fuselage and wrapped in foam rubber, you will never notice that the cell has been damaged without cycling the pack and seeing the dropoff in capacity. Monitor your charge current closely, and make sure that it doesn't exceed three times the C rate. C rate is 500 milliamps ($\frac{1}{2}$) for the 500 mAh batteries that are standard in radio systems, so you don't want to put more than 1 $\frac{1}{2}$ amps of charge current into your packs. A charger with a digital charge readout like the Leisure Digital really shines here.

You will seldom be able to get more than about an amp into your transmitter pack. This is because you are powering the charger from a 12-volt battery, and there isn't enough power available from the battery to fast charge more than seven cells. This doesn't mean you can't charge your transmitter, but you won't be able to bring it up to full charge. You will be able to put in enough for a couple more flights, though.

A digital voltmeter will help keep your system safe when field charging. The voltage of a battery pack climbs consistently when it is accepting a charge. When the voltage peaks and begins to drop, the pack is fully charged and the charge current is being converted to heat. If you have a digital voltmeter monitoring the pack voltage, you will spot this voltage peak and can stop charging before anything gets damaged.

There are several products that will field charge your transmitter and receiver safely and automatically. Bell Rock Industries has even developed a solar panel that charges your radio system. It works at a charge rate that won't damage your system if it is overcharged. The idea is to leave your transmitter and receiver plugged into the "Joose-Booster" system while you're not flying. It uses solar cells to keep your batteries topped off.

TRC Engineering makes an interesting field fast charger. It automatically selects its output voltage, so will charge packs of from one to ten cells. It puts out plenty of current, so really isn't designed for cells smaller than 500 mAh; but for those cells and larger, it really does the job.

The field charger that I use the most is the Ace RC FFC. This unit is completely automatic, and works on all standard four-cell receiver and eight-cell transmitter packs. You plug the FFC into your cigar lighter, and connect the plugs to the charging jacks on your system. When you switch the FFC on, it goes to a fast charge rate, indicated by lighted LEDs on the charger. It watches the voltage of both the transmitter and receiver. When it hits preset voltage levels, it switches to slow charge. It will switch over when your transmitter is about 50 percent charged, and your receiver about 80 percent. This gives you plenty of safety margin; more time on the FFC at the slow charge rate will bring the packs up farther.

There are two features I particularly like about the FFC. For one thing, it has circuitry that detects air temperature and adjusts the voltage cutoff accordingly. This helps prevent a problem that might happen on a sunny, hot day at the field. If your battery pack is very warm, fast charging it could build up enough heat to cause damage before the voltage rises far enough to trip the charger. Secondly, the FFC has a regulator on the input voltage source. This means that the fact that your car battery goes to about 14 volts when your motor is running won't damage the FFC or change the charge rate. So if you get surprised by a beautiful flying day and no airplanes charged, you have an answer. Put the plane in the car, connect the FFC, turn it on, and drive to the field. When you see the LEDs go out, you know your system has enough charge for a few flights.

Battery Testing Equipment. There are devices on the market that will make monitoring the condition of your batteries much easier. Some of them are intended to be used on the flying field, to see how much charge you have left in your system. These are commonly called ESVs or Expanded Scale Voltmeters. See Chapter 6 for descriptions of these and how to use them.

In your workshop, you can and should regularly test your system's batteries. The only way to get a good idea of how much capacity you have left in a battery is to drain it and measure the amount of current you get in the process. As we've discussed before, ni-cad cells are rated in terms of their useful capacity. Most radio systems use batteries rated at 500 milliamp-hours (mAh), meaning that they can supply 500 milliamps of current for an hour. So, theoretically, if you put a 500 milliamp load on one of these packs for an hour, it should be discharged to a normal level. You can measure the time it takes to discharge and have the capacity of the pack. Battery testers all work on this principle.

Before we go further, a couple of questions might have occurred to you. For one, what is this "normal level" to which a pack is discharged? Why not just flatten the pack right out?

As we discussed earlier, ni-cad batteries don't discharge in a linear fashion. They maintain a high level of voltage until they're just about discharged, and then drop abruptly. That dropoff point is the point that's important, since the batteries will run your radio up until they hit the dropoff. So a useful cycler will look for that point and stop timing when it sees it or before. The usual voltage cutoff level is 1.1 or 1.0 volts per cell.

It's also rather unhealthy to completely flatten a ni-cad cell consistently. It will reduce cell life. As the pack discharges deeply, one or two cells may go flat and be reverse-charged by the cells that are still pumping current through the pack. And if the flattened pack is not slow-charged after the deep discharge, the cells will charge at different rates and be out of balance.

The battery cycler I use the most is the Digipace, made by Ace RC. In fact, I have two of them, so I can test two systems at once. The Digipace is available in kit form, or assembled and tested. I've built mine from kits; although it's not a kit for the rank beginner, it's not a difficult assembly job.

The Digipace is capable of testing a four-cell receiver pack and a six, eight, or twelve-cell transmitter pack. It has a digital readout that displays the results of either pack, depending on where a switch is set. Another switch starts the test. To use the Digipace, you connect it to one or both packs. As soon as it's connected it functions as a standard-rate charger, charging the packs at the same rate as the charger that came with the radio. Push the switch, and the Digipace starts a clock and begins discharging the packs. When it senses that one of the packs has reached its discharge point, it stores the clock value. When the other pack reaches discharge, it stops the clock. You can read either time on the digital display. When it has the discharge time of either pack, it starts charging that pack. So you can turn it on, start the cycle, and come back in about 20 hours to a fully charged system that has been cycled and tested.

The Digipace reads out in minutes. Since it subjects the packs to the same loads they will encounter in typical use, this number of minutes is the time you can expect to use the system if you used it to its capacity. You can easily convert this number of minutes to milliamp/hours by using the formula in the Digipace instructions. Once you do this, you will have a good idea of the health of your battery packs. If they consistently test out at or above their rated capacity in mAh, they're healthy and happy. For example, I just put the radio system in my Piper Cub on the Digipace, and the receiver pack tested to 535 mAh; since the cells are rated at 500 mAh, I know that they're doing fine.

If the Digipace shows that a pack has less capacity than it's rated for, test it again. Maybe it wasn't fully charged. If it consistently tests low, don't trust your valuable airplane to it! Something's wrong somewhere.

Another good use for the Digipace is to give you an idea how much charge there is left in your battery pack after a day's flying. At the end of a flying session, hook up the Digipace and let it discharge your packs and bring them back up to charge. Note the number of minutes you would have had left for that day's flying. If it's less than you expected, look for some reason why your plane is soaking up more battery current than it ought to. Are your controls binding, or stalling your servos? Are your connectors all clean and free from corrosion? An early warning of these conditions can save your plane; it has for me!

One final note about the Ace Digipace: If you'd prefer that the readout show the capacity of the pack (in mAh) rather than the discharge time (in minutes), there's a way to modify the circuit board to do this. Ace sells a little kit with instructions and parts to do it.

TROUBLESHOOTING YOUR SYSTEM

Batteries account for 90 percent of the problems that people experience with radio control systems. A basic rule to keep in mind is to replace your ni-cad batteries every three years. No matter how they are charged, stored or cycled, batteries will deteriorate over time. The chemicals inside lose their potency. Changing them is cheap insurance. You can get more information on ni-cad batteries earlier in this chapter, or in Chapter 1 of *The Advanced Guide to Radio Control Sport Flying* (TAB Book #3060). Meanwhile, if your batteries are not your problem, where should you look?

Your connectors are the first suspect. Most have gold-plated contacts to help fight off corrosion. Inspect each of them under a magnifying glass. You can clean them with a stiff wire brush; do it carefully and use a small amount of rubbing alcohol. Turn on the system and wiggle each connector, looking for jittering servos. If you get an "Aha!" replace the connector and see if the problem goes away.

Check your switch harness. Test the action of the switch. It should give a solid snap. If it slides stiffly, there's dirt and oil inside. Replace the whole switch harness if you discover a bad switch.

Is the battery pack wrapped with plastic or PVC tape? This tape will "sweat" and can cause corrosion. Heat shrink wrapping is best; since it has no adhesive, it doesn't cause this problem. If you have to make a new pack or replace cells in an old one, use hot-melt glue to hold the cells together. You can buy the same heat-shrink material the factory uses to protect battery packs; RC car racers use it. Check your hobby store.

When you cut off a suspect connector, strip the wires a bit and inspect them. Sometimes the fine copper wire in radio leads will corrode and turn black. This "black wire syndrome" shows up every now and then, usually on the leads from the battery pack into the switch harness. It is an indication that the system may have been subjected to too much moisture somewhere along the line. All the wiring needs to be replaced. If you see blackened, corroded wires coming out of a battery pack or a switch harness, replace the whole harness. If you see them coming out of a receiver, send it in for servicing!

The servo is the part of an RC system that does the actual work. The receiver tells it how much to move. A pushrod is connected to a hole in the servo output wheel. The pushrod moves the control surface of the plane. (Photo courtesy Futaba)

For ultra-small RC models, Cannon makes these Super Micro Servos. You can almost hide one behind a quarter! (Photo courtesy *Model Retailer* magazine)

Sometimes a radio system will act just fine in shop and ground tests, then start to go nutty when the engine is fired up. Before flying a new machine, or after a crash or major modification, you should range test the system (on the field, in the same spot as you customarily test, as described in Chapter 6) with the engine running. A friend is essential for this job. You can range test by yourself if the plane is secured in a sturdy cradle or tied down to the ground, but it won't be as good a test. You're looking for the point when the servos start to jitter, and you have to be standing close to the plane to detect this over the noise of the engine. Never range test the system with the engine running without firmly securing the plane! Since you're deliberately trying to exceed the range of the radio, you're risking a runaway plane if you do this. The same applies to electric-powered planes; always range test them with the motor switched off, or while someone else is holding them!

If you find that your range is substantially reduced with the motor running, look for places in the plane where two metal parts are touching each other. Metal parts that are in occasional contact will create interference. The most common place for this to happen is the throttle arm that connects to the throttle servo pushrod. If the arm is metal and you use a metal clevis, you're asking for it. Swap it for a nylon clevis. Loose muffler screws or engine bolts are another common cause of metal-to-metal interference. Look everywhere.

If you eliminate this as a cause of interference, then there is a loose connection somewhere in your airborne system. Try another switch harness. Sometimes switches will get worn to the point where engine vibration will cause them to open up. Check the connectors as described above.

If everything passes this fine-tooth comb inspection and your system still jitters when the engine starts, you have a more serious problem that a technician needs to look at. It can be anything from a loose solder joint on the receiver's printed circuit board to a crack in the receiver crystal. A trip to the service center will cost you some flying time and a few bucks, but skipping it might well cost you an airplane or worse. When in doubt, send it in! The confidence is worth what you pay for it, and more.

SENDING A RADIO IN FOR SERVICE

You should return your radio for service when it has a problem that you can't track down. But that in itself isn't enough. If you're the kind of driver who waits until something goes wrong to have your car serviced, you know what it can cost you. A radio control system is just like a car, a stereo, or a VCR; it requires periodic maintenance. This is especially important after 1988, when more new frequencies open up. Old, out-of-tune radios will splatter onto new channels and cause all sorts of problems. On the other hand, older systems that are properly maintained will be usable for years to come. This is another reason not to buy the cheapest radio system you can find!

I make it a policy to send my radios in for service at least once every three years. I do this with all of them, because I don't have any airplanes that I particularly care to crash. A typical service call will cost less than $50, and I get back a radio that has been gone over by experts and had its electronics tested. It's the cheapest way to get a sense of security I know of.

When you finally decide to return a radio for servicing, there are a few basic rules you should follow. They will save time for the repairman, which can save you a lot of money.

If you have saved the original box the radio came in, it'll make an ideal shipping container. It can also give the repairman important information about the specific make and model of your system. Keep the boxes.

If you don't have the original box, find one that is plenty big enough for the whole system. Unscrew the transmitter antenna. Remove the switch and servos from the plane. Don't send in broken pieces of the model, you'll get plenty of sympathy without them. Put all parts in plastic bags. Now pack the components in the box, shielded with foam "popcorn" or wrapped in foam padding similar to the padding you use to protect the receiver when you install it in the plane. It'll be subject to the same kind of abuse when the shipper gets his hands on it. No part of the radio should be in contact with any part of the box.

Return the entire system: transmitter, receiver, receiver battery pack, and all servos. You never know where in the system a problem can come from . . . and if you only send in part of the system, what do you do if they can't find the problem? I know it's a pain to pull all the servos out of the plane, but if the problem turns out to be one of those servos, how are you going to know which one is guilty? Give the inquiring serviceman as many clues to the mystery as possible.

Write a note detailing the trouble you're having and the tests you have already performed. If you can save the repairman having to redo tests you've already done, that means a lower charge on your bill.

Include a check to cover return postage of the system. Depending on the service center you work with, they may require your approval of an estimate before they go ahead with the work. Make sure your phone numbers—daytime and evening—are on the note and in the box. While you're at it, put your name on your transmitter somewhere. You should have done this when you first bought it, but we forget so often.

A good service center will send you a postcard when they receive your system. They'll tell you when you can expect to hear from them. Give them as long as they ask for; it should seldom be more than a few weeks.

AM, FM, OR PCM?

Before 1981, only AM transmissions were allowed for radio control use by the Federal Communications Commission. When AMA petitioned the FCC for more RC frequencies, one of the things they asked for was an end on restriction on the type of modulation broadcast. They got it, and we have benefited from the introduction of new radio systems with more possibilities. From this has also come a lot of confusion over the question: Which is best?

Guess what? There's no easy answer. None of them is the answer to all our prayers; there is no such thing as a crashproof RC system. Each has advantages and disadvantages.

AM radios tend to be less expensive than FM systems, and considerably less so than PCM. AM has been in use for a lot of years. AM circuitry is tested and reliable, and there's plenty of it.

FM has the advantage that a receiver can be designed to capture the signal, just like the receiver in your car. However, if it loses capture, it can have more of a problem than AM in regaining it. FM technology has been gaining rapidly on AM, since there were many proven foreign FM systems ready to hit the American market. FM receivers still tend to be sensitive to splatter from poorly-tuned AM transmitters. Until some of the older AM systems reach the end of their useful lives and get thrown out, you should be aware of the possibility of trouble.

PCM is something completely different. The receiver incorporates a microcomputer which listens for digital signals from the matching transmitter. The transmitter incorporates a signature code in each frame of data it sends. If the receiver hears a signal frame without this identifying code, it ignores the data. This means that the receiver will be unaffected by interference, and the controls will stay in their previous position. If it's completely overwhelmed by the foreign signal, or if the transmitter is turned off, PCM receivers can be designed to go to a default "fail safe" mode. This means that instead of going crazy, like a conventional receiver, in this circumstance, the PCM receiver moves all its servos to a preset position and stays there until it hears another signal from its transmitter.

PCM systems are expensive and more bulky than AM or FM systems. They also have a noticeable delay between the control input and servo motion. It's less than half a second, but it's there. The receiver's computer takes that long to evaluate the incoming signal. The main axis controls (elevator, aileron, rudder) are updated first, so this is not a real problem in most aircraft. In fact, many pro aerobatics fliers have gone to PCM radios. They like the fact that the systems don't ever twitch, which makes for smoother flights. I have a PCM system that I use for valuable scale models. The only time I wouldn't use it is in a helicopter, where I like instant control response. This is simply a matter of personal preference, however; many world-class heli competitors use PCM radios.

INTERFERENCE

The AMA Frequency Committee has been extremely careful in designing a phase-in plan for the new frequencies. We have reached Phase Two, starting in 1988. The Committee has been carefully researching the effects of the introduction of new frequencies that happened in 1983.

When the subject of radio interference comes up, it seems you get hit from all sides by terms that only the electronics experts understand. At least, that's the way I feel. And it's a rare electron-pusher that will talk English for long enough to explain what's going on and whether or not you and I really need to give a darn about it.

There are several excellent books that go into great detail on the subject of radios and interference. You can get detailed information from AMA. Look in the Reference Section at the back of this book for copies of some of the AMA's info sheets on RC frequencies. For now, let's talk about the sort of interference that you might actually encounter on a typical Sunday flying session.

If you have a good, name-brand radio system that wasn't the cheapest one around, and you have charged the batteries and properly installed the system, you're not likely to see any kind of interference. You ought to be aware, however, of one potential interference source, commonly known as third-order intermodulation, or 3IM.

When two transmitters are operating at the same time on different frequencies, the radio energy they broadcast will interact. The two frequencies combine to produce "beat" frequencies a certain distance to one side or the other of each of the main signals. These products are of very low power, and never caused us trouble in the past when we only had six frequencies. This is because the old frequencies were spaced farther apart, and the beat frequencies popped up in between the frequencies that our receivers were listening for. Receivers didn't have to be designed to listen closely to one narrow part of the band (they were *wideband,* rather than *narrowband*).

Now we have 21 frequencies. Worse yet from an intermodulation standpoint, they're evenly spaced, 40 MHz apart. So when two signals from two transmitters produce beat frequencies, they sit right on two more of our new channels. This is the dreaded 3IM.

Disaster? Nope. The power of the beat frequencies are proportional to the distance between the two transmitters that are producing them. So, to reduce the 3IM beat frequencies, you separate the transmitters. If the pilots on the line are standing at least 20 feet apart, the 3IM signals are insignificant.

This is how it usually happens: Two pilots take off and are flying around merrily. A third pilot takes off, and he starts to notice that his system is twitchy. At certain points in the sky the plane dips or the throttle surges. He announces that he's having trouble, and the other two pilots offer advice. Sometimes they'll be standing right next to each other, each looking at his plane, trying to decide why this poor sucker is getting his derriere kicked all over the sky!

I've seen this happen a couple of times. I use the direct approach to deal with it: I holler "Spread out!" as soon as I realize what's happening. When the pilots move apart, control miraculously returns to the shaking thumbs of Pilot #3, and he lands.

This doesn't mean that Pilot #3 has a crummy radio. In all probability, when his radio was designed, intermodulation interference wasn't a problem. For a very large percentage of sport fliers, intermodulation may never be a problem. But as the number of fliers increases along with the number of frequencies, more and more of you will encounter it.

What Do You Do About It? You can deal with intermodulation interference simply, as described above, by being aware of it and avoiding conditions that cause it. Change your flight line to have marked positions for the pilots to stand.

You can buy a new receiver for your radio system that has good abilities to reject this kind of interference. The best systems I've found in this particular feature are the ones using dual conversion receivers.

You can use a simple formula to see what combination of frequencies will cause 3IM. Suppose two fliers are up, one on channel 44 and one on 42. These two frequencies will beat together and produce 3IM on two more frequencies, one above them and one below them. Which channels will the 3IM be on?

To find the channels that will be at risk, double one frequency and subtract the other from the result: 44 times two is 88. Subtract 42 and you get 46, which is one of the channels which can get hit. Now work it from the other side: 42 times 2 is 84, minus 44 gives you channel 40. So those two guys on the flight line can interfere with channels 40 and 46. Before you take off on one of these channels, make sure the other pilots are standing at least 15 feet apart to minimize the 3IM.

Testing Your System for Interference Rejection. AMA Frequency Committee member George Steiner has worked out some field tests you can use on the field to see how sensitive your system is to intermodulation interference.

To conduct George's tests, you need your airplane and transmitter, and two friends with their transmitters. One friend's transmitter must be on the same frequency as yours. The other friend's transmitter must be on a channel adjacent to yours; if you're on channel 44, you need another transmitter on channel 42 or 46. Incidentally, both of the Steiner Tests are performed with the transmitter antennas fully extended, just as if you were flying.

You also need a field with a line 100 feet long, marked in 10 foot increments. No one will mind if you do this at the flying field, if you tell them what it's all about!

The first of the Steiner tests is for adjacent channel rejection. Will your receiver operate properly with another person flying on the channel right next to you? Modern receivers certainly should. Here's how you can tell.

Turn on your receiver and put the plane down at one end of the 100 foot line. Go to the other end of the line with the friend who has the receiver on a channel next to yours. Both of you turn on your transmitters. Your receiver will be getting your signal clearly, and your servos won't jitter. Now put your transmitter on the ground at the 100 foot mark. Walk down the line toward your plane with your friend, carrying the transmitter on the adjacent channel. Watch for the point when your servos start to twitch and jitter.

You should be able to get within 30 feet of your plane before the servos start to twitch. A good receiver will still be solid if both of you are standing five to ten feet away. If things get twitchy at much over 30 feet, beware. Your system could need retuning.

The second Steiner Test looks for the ability of your receiver to reject interference on the channel it's listening to. This will give you an idea of how well it'll do when it's in an intermodulation (3IM) situation like the one we described earlier.

Put your plane down on one end of the 100 foot line, and turn on the receiver. Turn on your transmitter, and put it down on the line 20 feet away from your plane. It should be resting on its base, not on its back, with the antenna pointing up into the air.

Now send your friend with the transmitter on the same frequency as yours to the other end of the line and have him switch it on. As he walks down

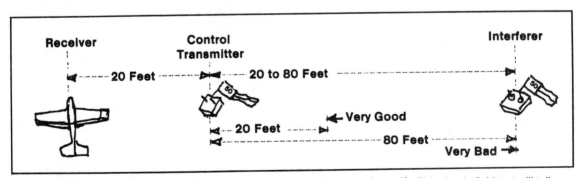

How well will your receiver reject interference from another signal on your channel? This simple field test will tell you. You need a transmitter that broadcasts on the same channel you're using. The closer it gets before you lose control of your system, the better your system is at rejecting interference. (Illustration courtesy *Model Aviation* magazine)

the line toward your plane, watch for the point at which the servos start to jitter. This will happen when your receiver is no longer able to filter out signals on your frequency that aren't coming from your transmitter.

If your friend can get to the 50 foot mark before your servos start to jump, your system is fine. A good receiver will be solid when your friend and his transmitter are only 30 feet away. If things get jumpy when he is much more than 50 feet away, things are not as solid as they should be. Think carefully about sending your system in for a checkup.

Chapter 4

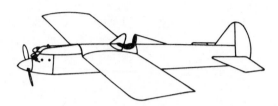

Trainer Airplanes and
Basic Construction Techniques

HERE ARE MANY AIRPLANE KITS THAT ARE DE-
scribed as "trainers." Most of them are fine
for the purpose, but you can't be certain. Every airplane flies differently, and every model pilot's skills
are different. If you're armed with a little basic
knowledge, you'll be able to find a first airplane that
you'll thoroughly enjoy.

WHERE TO GET YOUR FIRST AIRPLANE

There are two ways to buy model supplies: from
a hobby store, or through mail order. Buying from
a hobby dealer is much the better of the two. RC
modeling is something like the hobby of photogra-
phy; you will need a lot of help and advice to do it
successfully. The best place to get this help is at
your hobby shop. You can open up the kit and look
through it. You can get any accessories you need
right then and there. The dealer can recommend
covering, glue, and any special tools you might need.
If you have questions as you build the kit, you can
call him and get answers fast.

Mail order buying often offers you a lower price

than the hobby store, but there's a risk involved,
too. It's going to take a while to get your kit.
There's no one to call when you need help. You will
probably open the box and discover that you need
a fuel tank, an engine mount, pushrods. Finally, by
the time you've paid to have the product shipped
to you, the mail order price doesn't look as good
anymore.

If you live in an area without a good hobby shop,
then by all means consider buying mail order. I grew
up in a small town in upstate New York, and I knew
every page of the SIG Manufacturing and Estes Industries catalogs by heart. But when I went to college and discovered a hobby store nearby, I never
shopped anywhere else. I got to know the people,
and learned a lot from them. My hobby really
blossomed in those years, more than it had when
I was a loner. I'm still grateful to that store . . . and
to the stores I patronize in the city where I now live.

WHAT MAKES A GOOD TRAINER KIT?

Your first airplane should be easy to build

correctly—not necessarily easy to build, although that's nice, too. But getting a plane that is easy to build straight is worth a lot.

Look for full-size plans that show the shape of each part, so you can identify them easily.

The bigger the instruction book, the better. Few model kits have what I consider to be adequate instructions. Ask your hobby dealer to open the box and let you look at the instructions. If you come across a word or a procedure that you don't understand, *ask*. Don't be shy about it . . . that's his job.

For your first airplane, you should favor a model with a fuselage built up from balsa sheet, rather than one made of a framework of square balsa sticks. The framework fuselages are lighter and just as strong as the sheet types, but the sheet sides are much easier to construct. This is because of the extra attention you have to pay to getting the fuselage perfectly straight when you are joining framework sides with crossmembers. A sheet-sided fuselage will have the sides precut to the right length. Getting a straight fuselage will consist of gluing the firewall to the front edge of each side and the fuselage formers to the inside from the front to the back, then gluing the sheets together at the tail.

To Aileron or Not to Aileron? There's a debate raging among RC instructors about ailerons. Many insist that a beginner should start out with a three-channel airplane, those channels being rudder, elevator, and throttle. Such airplanes are usually docile, since they rely on a lot of *dihedral* (the angle of upsweep of the wing tips) for turning control. Dihedral also helps stabilize a plane in level flight, and make the plane self-recovering.

A self-recovering airplane will help you get out of a situation many beginners encounter. You lose your orientation in a turn. The plane's turning tightly, and you mistakenly move the stick to turn the plane even tighter in an attempt to level it out. This is called a spiral dive, for obvious reasons. Believe me, it's easier to get into than it sounds!

If you get into a spiral dive with a self-correcting airplane, you simply release the stick. The plane will come out of the turn, still coming down, but travel-

If you only have a small flying field, the Megowcoupe from Flyline Models might appeal to you. With an .049 engine for power, it flies very slowly. Construction might be a chore for a beginner. (Photo courtesy *Model Retailer* magazine)

ing straight. You can get your orientation back, and add up elevator to level it out again.

Planes without ailerons are generally simpler to build, since you don't have to hinge the ailerons, rig the linkages, or install the aileron servo. Of course, you don't have an aileron servo to plug in when you put the wing on the plane. And if you bought a radio system without servos, such as the Ace RC Olympic V, you only need to buy three servos to complete the plane.

Why Use Ailerons? On the other hand, you are probably going to want to fly a plane with ailerons at some point. Rudder-only planes aren't as precise as aileron ships, and they aren't capable of some maneuvers that the full-house four-channel jobs can perform. And if your model is scale or scale-like, a lot of dihedral angle in the wing is not aesthetically pleasing.

An airplane's rudder does not turn the plane. A plane can only turn by banking, lowering one wing. Rudder-only planes turn by making use of the high dihedral angle; when you add rudder, you roll the plane and force one wing down. A cleaner, smoother way to turn a model is to bank with aileron, and slowly add up elevator to pull the nose around in the direction of the bank. Then feed in opposite aileron to level the wings, letting the elevator return to neutral as you do. It might sound tricky, but it's a smooth, natural action. It lets you control the bank angle of the plane (with ailerons) and the diameter of the turn (with elevator) at all times.

So which one should you get? You decide. If you start out with rudder-only three-channel planes, you'll have to learn a new style of turning when you try an aileron ship. On the other hand, aileron ships will seldom level themselves out of a spiral dive. Which one you choose for your first or second trainer depends on what you feel comfortable with and which kit appeals to you most.

Please remember: Don't tackle the Mustang or Warhawk you want to build as your first kit! You'll almost certainly crash it. Pick a high-wing airplane; it's easier to keep oriented with a high-wing plane. Pick something that flies slowly. If you meet these two criteria, you can aileron or not as you please.

STARTING WITH SAILPLANES

If you want to start with something as easy as possible to fly, or you have to teach yourself, consider starting out with a sailplane. They fly more slowly than powered planes, so they're easier to stay ahead of. Since they have large wings, they're easier to keep in the air, they turn more gently, and they're more forgiving of a beginner's tendency to overcontrol. Since there's no engine, that's one less thing for you to get frustrated with. And, generally speaking, they're easy for a beginner to build.

Two-meter sailplanes are the most convenient size. A wing two meters long is easy to tuck into the back seat of a car. The wing panels won't be too big to build on your kitchen table, and you won't go broke buying covering for it.

The two most popular two-meter sailplane kits in my experience, are the Gentle Lady and the Olympic 650. The Gentle Lady is kitted by Carl Goldberg Models. It's a supremely friendly airplane, very easy to build and just as easy to fly. The instructions are illustrated at every step, and show you how to cover the model and install the radio. You can leave off the balsa nose piece of the Gentle Lady and put on an .049 engine if you like.

The Olympic 650 is kitted by Airtronics. Like other Airtronics kits, the quality is outstanding. Parts are sawn and sanded rather than die-cut, and all the necessary hardware is included. The Oly 650 performs better in light air than the Gentle Lady, and can be a competitive ship in the hands of an expert.

Sailplanes make excellent training planes, since most fly slowly and gently. This is the Pussycat from Bob Martin RC Models. It's an easy kit for the first-timer to build and fly. (Photo courtesy *Model Retailer* magazine)

The Robbe Windy is really a powered sailplane. It can take off from the ground, cruise up to altitude, and glide around at a low throttle setting. The fuselage is molded plastic, and the wing is sheeted foam. (Photo courtesy Robbe USA)

Another popular two-meter sailplane is the Metrick, kitted by Top Flite Models. This is a real performer, a contest-quality design. The detailed instructions make it suitable as a first model.

If you like the flying characteristics of a sailplane but still want a powered model, see Chapter 1 of *The Advanced Guide to Radio Control Sport Flying* (TAB Book #3060). There are several sailplane-like designs that are available for electric power; the most popular is the Electra kit from Carl Goldberg Models. Electrics are not much more trouble than sailplanes, because you won't have trouble getting the motor started.

BASIC BUILDING TECHNIQUES

Before you start fitting parts together, lay them all out and identify them. Write each part's name on the part with a soft lead pencil. If you use a felt-tip pen for this, make sure you don't mark on any part that will be on the outside of the plane. Felt-tip ink will soak right through many finishes, even iron-on coverings!

Read the instructions until you have a good grasp of them. Look at the plans as you do, and work out each construction step in your mind. You'll be-

gin to develop an ability to "read" plans, visualizing the construction steps. It's often very difficult to spell out in words some construction detail that can be shown in a drawing. Look for detail drawings of the difficult parts.

In the course of studying the plans and laying out the parts, you'll locate the construction steps that look the most difficult to you. It's useful to test-fit the parts together without glue until you have a good idea of how they fit and where they go. It'll build your confidence later.

Cutting Balsa Wood

Balsa wood is amazing stuff. It's remarkably strong, especially against its grain. It's relatively soft and can be cut and shaped easily. But its great virtue as far as we're concerned is its light weight. Years ago, when I worked for a company that manufactured model rocket kits, we bought balsa by the plank. The planks were two feet wide, a foot thick, and eight to ten feet long. I could carry two on each shoulder. You can imagine what the neighbors thought when we unloaded the lumber truck and tossed the planks into a second-story loft door!

Balsa is so light because it is formed of fibers

held together in a honeycomb-like structure. Because of this, it can be crushed easily. This makes it extremely important to use *sharp* tools to cut balsa. I have several different knives that I favor for different jobs. They all have replaceable blades, and I have spares handy. The common X-Acto #11 blade, the one that tapers to a sharp point, can be bought in boxes of 50 in art supply stores. This is what I use for most work. Since the blades are cheap, it's easy to have one knife handle with a new blade for precision work and another with an older blade for hacking.

For precision work and very light wood, many people use single-edged razor blades. These are fine, but I find them difficult to grip comfortably. *Model Builder* magazine markets a knife called Uber Sciver which is just as sharp as a razor blade if not sharper. Its handle uses a drawbar clutch that is tightened from the rear, so it doesn't loosen when you cut around curves. The handle is hex-shaped so it doesn't roll. I love 'em for precision work. The compound edge of the blade is easily honed with a Peck-Polymers Sharpy tool. The only drawback that I've found is that Uber Sciver blades are relatively fragile. Save them for close work, and don't flex or twist the blade.

You'll also want to have a razor saw. These saws have very thin blades and small teeth, and will cut the hardest balsa easily. I have several different sizes in my shop. The small ones are good for close work, and the small blades are easier to keep from bending. Larger blades are needed to cut through balsa blocks or thicker strip stock.

You'll also need a good surface to cut on. You can use your building board, but it will wear out that much quicker. I have a square block of hard black rubber that has been finished to a flat surface. It keeps small parts from slipping and protects the knife blade when it goes through the wood. I found this block at a store that specializes in model railroad supplies; ask your hobby dealer if he has them in his railroad department.

Fitting Cut Parts

The difference between a strong, smooth fuselage or wing and a weak, irregular one can be summed up in one word: *patience*. You must cultivate the patience necessary to fit each part to each other as closely as you can. Once you're in the habit, you'll find that fitting the parts into the structure as perfectly as you can is one of the great pleasures of model building.

If you're working with die-cut parts, be careful as you sand their edges smooth. Die-cut parts are usually made with a little margin for fine sanding and smoothing. Be careful that you don't sand them smaller than they need to be.

Parts that have to be cut to length or to shape should always be cut slightly oversized. As a friend of mine says, "You can't cut it longer!" Cut the part and test-fit it, noting where it needs to be sanded to shape. Then sand it lightly with fine grit paper, no more than four or five strokes before you test-fit the part again. If you accidentally sand the part too far, *do not* try to bridge the gap with glue! It might appear to work, but will return to haunt you later. Look for a place where your too-short part will fit. For example, if you're building a framed fuselage and one of your crossmembers comes out too short, look toward the tail of the plane for a spot that needs a shorter crossmember. Obviously, you should always cut the longer parts first.

If there is no place to use the too-small part, you can build up the surface you oversanded with a small piece of scrap wood. Make a good glue joint, and shape the new piece to conform with the old one. Then test-fit again, shaping more slowly this time.

Engine Mounts

Engines are mounted in one of two ways. The engine can be bolted to hardwood rails that extend forward from the fuselage into the nose. These engine rails are built into the structure of the fuselage and provide a very solid mount. But you must plan the engine you will mount before the fuselage construction is completed, and changing to an engine of a different size is difficult.

The most common method of engine mounting is to bolt the engine to an engine mount, which is bolted to the firewall. These engine mounts can be made from aluminum or glass-reinforced nylon. The aluminum mounts sometimes come predrilled and

Great Planes Models makes a series of trainer and sport kits. The Super Sportster is an excellent trainer for a modeler who is ready to try aerobatics. (Photo courtesy *Model Retailer* magazine)

tapped for a particular engine. These are the best kinds of mounts you can buy, but they require that you change the whole mount if you ever decide to use a different engine. You will find aluminum engine mounts made by Tatone, J'Tec, C.B. Associates, and SIG Manufacturing in your hobby shop. If he doesn't have the particular mount you need, it can be ordered quickly.

Nylon engine mounts are perfectly strong and durable. They usually come in widths rather than drilled for a particular engine. This is handy, since one mount will fit a range of different engines. They're also considerably less expensive than the cast aluminum mounts.

Nylon engine mounts have one other advantage that I like. Instead of having to drill holes in the mount and tap them for bolts, the motor can be securely mounted with self-tapping wood screws. Position the engine on the mount, checking to make sure it fits properly without spreading the arms and is in the proper position along the length of the arms.

Now use a pencil to mark the positions of the engine mounting lug holes. Remove the engine. Drill pilot holes through the mount arms; use a drill that is smaller in diameter than the screws you will attach the engine with. When you mount the engine, the screws will tap themselves into the nylon. It grips the threads tightly. There's not much chance that you will strip out the holes by overtightening the screws unless you drilled them too large in the first place.

Any engine mount should be bolted through the firewall with bolts threaded into blind nuts. Blind nuts are small nuts with points around the outside that imbed themselves in the wood to hold the nut in position. You should fit these mounts while you still have access to the back of the firewall.

Pushrods

Pushrods connect the control surfaces of the plane to the servo output arms. There are two types of pushrods: *rigid rods* and *flexible rods* or cables.

Rigid Pushrods. Rigid pushrods are usually hard balsa. Some kits include fiberglass pushrods; even graphite arrow shafts have been used with great success. They are most often used for elevators and ailerons, since there's plenty of room for them to stick straight inside the back of the fuselage behind the radio compartment.

Rigid pushrods must be fitted with wires on each end to connect to the control surfaces. These wires are usually threaded on one end, so that a clevis can be screwed on. For details of how to connect these to the control surfaces, see the information on radio installation below.

The easiest way to attach a threaded rod to the end of a rigid pushrod starts with the bending of the non-threaded end of the rod at a right angle. The bent part of the rod should project downward no farther than the width of the rigid rod to which it will be fitted. Now drill a hole through the rigid rod about an inch from the end, for this bent end to stick into. Cut a V-shaped notch from this hole to the end of the rod. This notch should be deep enough that the wire can lay in it flush with the surface of the rod when the bent end is inserted into the hole. Use medium-grade CyA glue to glue the bent wire in place. Now wrap some thread around the end of the pushrod, from behind the hole to the end. Flood this with thin CyA glue. When it sets, the rod will be firmly in place and there'll be no chance of splitting the rod because of the notch you cut in it.

Flexible Pushrods. Flexible rods are sold in hobby shops in different lengths. The brand I use most often is Gold-N-Rod, from Sullivan Products. It's sold in several different grades, from a thick, fairly stiff rod for heavy duty applications to a thinner more flexible rod for going around corners.

Flexible rods consist of a plastic tube and an inner rod that slides within it. The inner rod connects to the servo arm and control surface, and does the actual work. The outer tube supports the rod throughout its length so it doesn't flex when pushed. The inner rod is actually a tube, and it connects to the control surfaces with short lengths of threaded rod that are screwed into each end. Clevises are then threaded onto the rods. This gives you a

pushrod that you can adjust at either end by threading the clevises in or out.

The most important thing to remember when installing flexible rods is to secure the outer tube firmly at several points along its length. This is especially important in places where the rod goes around curves or corners. If the tube isn't secure, the rod can flex into these curves and not push the way it should.

Outer pushrod tubing can be glued into ribs and bulkheads with CyA glue if it's roughened with sandpaper first. Cut holes in the bulkheads that the outer tube can fit through easily. Sand the rod lightly and run it through the holes. Apply medium grade CyA at each joint.

If you're going to use flexible rods in the wing, it's best to plan where they will fit through the ribs and drill them all at once. This makes sure that the holes are properly aligned, and saves you a lot of trouble trying to cut holes in the ribs when they're held rigidly in the wing.

I use flexible rods for almost all applications. The only drawback I've ever discovered is the fact that the plastic rods will expand and contract with changes in temperature. This will sometimes show up after you bring the plane out of your cool basement and leave it sitting in the sun for a few hours. Check your control surfaces before you fly, and readjust the clevises if necessary.

Hinges

There are a lot of different hinging methods available. Most kits come with hinges included, but few instructions on just how to deal with them. This doesn't mean they're not important: they can affect the flyability of the plane and the life of the battery pack and servos.

The most important thing I've found in making good hinges is to have the parts to be hinged properly shaped. Look at the plans. There will be a cross-section drawing of the control surface that shows how it should be shaped. If it's an aileron, the hinge will probably be inserted at the narrowest point of the surface up near the top. If it's a rudder or elevator, the hinge goes into the center of the surface's edge, which has been rounded. Sand the surface until

The new AeroStar 40 from Midwest Products is designed for the first-time flier. The instruction manual (over 100 pages long!) takes you through every step of building and covering. (Photo courtesy *Model Retailer* magazine)

you get it to the shape shown on the plans, no matter how long it takes. It'll pay off.

Types of Hinges. The most common hinges these days are made of nylon plastic. They come in different shapes and sizes. The actual hinge is usually a thin place in the middle of the plastic piece. You might not think this is very strong—but just try to rip one apart.

It's a good idea to "break in" these hinges by flexing them a few times. You can feel the difference between a brand-new hinge and one that has been flexed.

Pinned Hinges. Many hinges have small pins in them, just like a door hinge. These are very strong and usually aren't as stiff as the solid hinges described above.

The only thing to be cautious of with this kind of hinge is encountered when installing them. If you're a little sloppy with the glue, especially CyA

glue, you can glue the hinge solid. There are several simple methods to prevent the glue from getting into the hinge. Some builders will warm up a little Vaseline in a dish until it becomes liquid, fold the hinge in half, and dip the hinge pin in the Vaseline. Others use light oil, preferably in a pinpoint oiler; these are commonly sold for model trains. Whatever method you use, the idea is to coat the pin of the hinge with something that will keep the glue from sticking to it, while not preventing the glue from making a solid bond to the rest of the hinge.

Installing Hinges. Hinging can be an irritating job. If you're not careful you can split the wood you're working on, and if you don't get the cut properly centered, the hinge might bind up. But if you follow a few simple procedures, you'll find that the job is going easily and you wind up with a smoothly working control surface.

The most important task is to slot the edges

where the hinge will be inserted. It's important to get the slots centered in the edge, so the two pieces will be properly aligned. Also, if one hinge is out of line, you will often feel a distinct binding or tendency to hang up at one point as you move the control surface up and down.

Carl Goldberg Models makes a little gizmo called a Hinge Slotting Guide. It's a D-shaped piece of plastic that has two little tabs on the ends of the flat side. There's a small point in the middle of this flat surface. You hold the flat surface up against the surface to be slotted, and turn it slightly so that the two tabs rest on the top and bottom of the surface. Now, when you move the tool along the surface, that little point scores a line down the precise center of the surface. It isn't very deep, but you can see it.

The next step is to lay the two surfaces to be hinged side-by-side, aligned as you want them to be after the hinges are installed. Mark them with a soft lead pencil (ink can show through the paint or covering) where you want to install the hinges. Check the plans; they'll usually show you the best places to put the hinges.

What you do next depends on the type of hinges you're installing. Most hinges are flat, so you'll need to cut a slot in the surface along the line you've marked. Cut it a little wide so you can move the hinge from side to side before gluing it in place. This will allow you to get the hinged surfaces in proper alignment before gluing the hinges in.

Using a thin-bladed knife, such as an X-Acto #11 or an Uber Sciver, slip it into the surface along the mark you made and work it back and forth. Now work the knife into the slot a second time, making it wide enough to slip the hinge in. You might like to use a wider-bladed knife for this. The idea is to make the slot wide enough that inserting the hinge won't crack the wood.

If your hinge has a pin, the parts that hold the pin in the center are slightly wider than the main body of the hinge. In order for the hinge to fit flush, you need to cut a small V-shaped slot along the outer edges of the cut you just made. This will allow the pinned area of the hinge to tuck all the way into the wood, and the two hinged pieces will fit together with little or no gap. Test-fit the pieces several times until you have this right. If you've lubricated the hinge pin, the glue won't stick to it when you finally glue the hinge in.

Several hinges have a round shaft in the part that fits into the slot. These "hinge points" are a little easier to install than flat hinges. Instead of cutting a slot, you make a hole by twirling a drill bit with your fingertips into the wood at the right spot. The round shaft on the hinge body has raised ridges. When you squirt glue into the hole and insert the hinge shaft, it makes a secure bond that doesn't need to be pinned.

Once the slots or holes are properly cut and you have the hinges in place but not glued, work the surface up and down a few times to make sure that everything is aligned properly. Now, decide how you want to glue the hinges in. Have you already covered the surfaces? If so, go ahead and glue them in. If the surfaces haven't been covered yet, you should either not glue the hinges in yet, or glue in only one side. Separating the surfaces will make covering a lot easier.

I like to use medium-grade CyA glue (Super Jet, Zap-a-Gap, Hot Stuff Super T, etc.) to install hinges. It gives you a minute to get the hinge in and properly positioned. Many people use thin CyA (Hot Stuff, Zap, Jet, etc.), put on the hinge joint after the hinge is in place. The thin CyA wicks into the wood and makes a bond. This is okay for small surfaces, but I prefer to be sure of getting glue into the joint between the hinge and the wood.

After all the hinges are glued, you should pin them. Pinned hinges won't separate from the surface without tearing out the wood they're secured to. I push regular straight pins into the top of the surface, through the hinge, and out the other side. I clip off one side of the pin flush with the surface (or as close to flush as I can get) with a pair of diagonal cutters, then I push this cut end down into the wood a little farther. Now I clip off the other end, and push this end into the wood too. This leaves me with a pin that is recessed into the wood at both ends, so it won't stick up and scratch things or make a bump in the covering.

D-Hinges. I've had very good success with a product called D-Hinges. They're made by Model Products Corporation, and most hobby shops carry them. For most hinging applications, they're excellent. They are no harder to install than standard hinges, and are by far the smoothest and least-binding hinges I've ever used. As an added benefit, you can easily remove the control surface at any time, even after the plane is built.

D-Hinges come in several sizes. You buy the size that matches the thickness of the surface you're working with. You can't get them smaller than ⅛ inch, which will fit most common RC kits.

Each D-Hinge has two parts. One glues to the solid surface, the other to the movable surface. Both are cast from a special plastic that can be bonded by common CyA glues. One part is shaped like a D, with a lengthwise slot in the curved side. The other part consists of two small D-shapes with a square bar between them. These parts fit together to form the hinge, with the bar inserted through the lengthwise slot in the other piece. The bar is shaped so that it will only fit through the slot when the two pieces are 90 degrees to each other.

To install D-Hinges, you first slice a square strip from the edge of the control. If the surface is ⅛ inch thick, you remove a ⅛ by ⅛ strip from it. Set it aside for use later. I use a Master Airscrew Balsa Stripper for this step, but a metal straightedge will work. If the control surface is a built-up structure rather than a solid sheet, you can skip this step, but get a piece of square strip stock the same thickness as the surface.

Mark your hinge locations, and glue the hinges in position. As I said, they are made of special plastic that is designed to be bonded with CyA glue. It doesn't really matter which piece is where, as long as you have mating pairs across from each other. I put the pairs together and glue them to the surfaces while the whole thing is resting on a flat surface. If you accidentally glue the hinges solid, a little Debonder will free them.

The instructions tell you to put the hinge piece in place and put a drop of thin CyA on the joint. I prefer to put a drop of gap-filling CyA (Super Jet, Zap-a-Gap, etc.) on the hinge piece and press it in place on the surface.

Once all the pieces are together, disconnect the surfaces by turning them at 90 degrees to each other. Use the strip you cut off the movable surface to fill in the spaces between the hinge pieces on that surface. Since it was cut from there, it should fit smoothly back into place by removing pieces of it to fit around the hinge pieces. Lightly sand the strip to get the corners round, the same cross-section as the hinge pieces. *Voila:*—a perfectly hinged surface.

Making Hinges out of Covering Material. If the control surfaces are very thin (like ¹⁄₁₆ inch) or your airplane is intended for slow flight, you can make hinges from the covering material itself while you're covering. I especially like Micafilm for this because of its very high tear resistance, but any popular covering will work just fine. Friends of mine use this hinging method exclusively, making hinges from MonoKote that last for the life of the plane. I don't recommend it for fast aerobatics or racing planes, but for most sport models it will work just fine.

Suppose you're covering an elevator and want to hinge it to the stabilizer. First, cover the bottom of the stabilizer. Now lay a sheet or strip of ¹⁄₁₆ thick balsa or cardboard on top of the stab, with its edge flush with the edge of the stab to be hinged to the elevator. Now lay the elevator on top of this spacer sheet, aligning the edge to be hinged with the edges of the sheet and the stab. Pick up this sandwich and check again that the surfaces are properly aligned. Now iron the covering onto these edges, and over the top onto what will be the bottom of the elevator. Make sure the covering is stuck to the edges firmly and completely, with no gaps.

Flip the elevator over so that it is even with the stab, resting on your building board. There is now a double layer of covering separating the two pieces, stuck to both, and a small ridge of covering sticking up above this line. Remove the spacer sheet and iron a single sheet of covering material over the top surfaces of both stab and elevator. You might have to run your iron over the joint between the pieces a couple of times to make sure it's smooth. If the two pieces move apart slightly, no matter. *Voila* once again:—a hinge made of two sheets of covering stuck to each other, with no gaps down the length of the hinge line.

The only thing that can go wrong with this process is improper shaping of the mating surfaces. If they are both square so that they close against each other when pushed together, the surface will be able to hinge upward but not downward. For an aileron, where the mating surface is undercut at an angle to allow downward movement, there's no problem with this method. If you have an elevator and stab, as in the example above, it's best to shape the leading edge of the elevator to a triangular cross-section with the point touching the center of the trailing edge of the stab. This is easier to stick the covering to and will give plenty of movement in both directions. Simply rounding the leading edge of the elevator may not be adequate.

INSTALLING THE RADIO SYSTEM

You've usually finished and covered the plane before you begin to install the radio system. Check the instructions; this might vary with your kit. But the engine will be in place, and all the control surfaces hinged and with the control horns in position.

Switch Harness

The first thing to consider is where to locate the receiver on-off switch and charging jack. The rule here is to put the switch in a convenient place on the opposite side of the fuselage from the engine's exhaust pipe. Exhaust oil can quickly get into a switch and cause it to fail—not to mention working its way in under the covering around the switch hole!

I prefer to use a switch that comes with a faceplate of some sort, so you can cut the hole slightly oversize and it'll cover it up. Most switches that come with radio systems are like this. You can use the faceplate to draw lines to mark where to cut the hole. Position it at an appropriate spot, and mark through the switch hole and the two screw holes

with a sharp lead pencil. Now you should be able to use a #11 blade and a small drill bit to make the holes.

When you position the switch, put it where it won't interfere with pushrods or servos on the inside of the plane. I like to put it on the side of the fuselage, under the wing if it's a high-wing plane. It should be in a spot where it's easy to tell at a glance whether or not the receiver is switched on or off. I like to put a small drop of white paint on the ''on'' side of the switch faceplate to make it obvious.

You don't have to mount the battery charging jack on the outside of the plane, but it comes in handy. With the jack permanently mounted on the outside, you won't have to remove the wing to check the batteries on the field. It also makes it easier to hook up your charger, if you hang your airplanes from the basement ceiling, as I do.

Most radio systems come with a charging jack that includes a faceplate similar to the one that came with the receiver switch. Check your radio's instructions for specifics. Ace RC sells some jacks for this purpose that have faceplates. Ernst Mfg. sells a jack holder that fits Futaba radio systems. Some radio manufacturers have special switch harnesses that you can buy with these features. The neatest one I've seen is from Multiplex; the switch and charge jack are in a single unit. A sliding door covers the jack, and the whole thing fits nearly flush with the surface of the fuselage. Nifty!

Receiver Battery

Your receiver battery is often the heaviest thing in the airplane, after the engine. This comes in handy when you want to add nose weight. Why give a piece of lead a free ride, when you can have nose weight that earns its keep?

In any case, check your plane's center of gravity before installing the receiver battery. It should balance near the CG shown on the plans. If it balances forward of this location, you don't need nose weight and you should install the receiver pack close to the CG. If it balances at or behind the location shown on the plans, install the pack as far forward as you can get it. This might mean putting it under the fuel tank.

Most radio systems come with a battery pack in a "square" configuration, i.e., two pairs of cells side by side. This is fine for most airplanes. But if you need to tuck the pack underneath the fuel tank, there might not be enough room. A "flat pack" is the answer. Flat packs have all four cells side by side. Most radio manufacturers offer flat packs as an option. Ace RC sells receiver packs in every imaginable shape, either shrink-wrapped or in plastic boxes. You just attach connectors for your particular system, and you're on your way.

Wherever the receiver pack is installed, it needs to be wrapped in foam rubber. Make sure this is vibration-absorbing foam, rather than the popcorn-type stuff used in packing crates. The idea is to isolate the electronics from the engine vibration. True, the battery pack is a lot less susceptible to vibration than other electronic equipment, such as the receiver. But that doesn't mean you can just stick it to the fuselage bottom with double-sided tape! This is another lesson I learned the hard way, when my Gee Bee Model D flew itself into the ground. The vibration had loosened a wire that was soldered to the battery pack, which cleverly turned off the receiver just as I was banking onto final approach. I've wrapped my batteries in foam rubber ever since.

Pushrod Installation

If you didn't do it before, now's the time to figure out where your pushrods go. If you used flexible pushrods, you built them in as you finished the rear of the fuselage, supporting the outer tubes at every bulkhead. If your kit calls for wooden pushrods, make them up now. Cut them to the length shown on the plans, and install the threaded rods longer than they will need to be. It's a lot easier to make them shorter than longer!

Put the pushrods into the fuselage and connect them to the control surfaces. You may have to do a little rebending of the threaded rods to get the installation just right. The pushrods should not seat against each other at any point along their length. Once you have these in, you can see where your

servos need to go.

Servo Mounting

There are two common ways to mount servos in the fuselage. You can use a plastic servo tray. These are often included with the radio system. They have holes that fit the servos and some sort of setup to hold them in place. The tray itself is mounted to two hardwood rails glued into the fuselage.

The other method is to mount the servos to the rails directly without using a tray. This is a little trickier than using the tray, since the rails have to be properly positioned to allow the servos to fit in the right positions.

Whichever method you use, be sure the mounting rails are firmly glued to the fuselage sides. My usual practice is to glue them in with regular-grade CyA glue, a drop on the end of each rail. Then I finish rigging the pushrods until I'm certain that I won't need to move the servos. If they do have to be moved, I use a debonding agent (Z-7 Debonder, Jet De-Solv, etc.) to free the rails and reposition them. When I'm sure it's in the right spot, I cut eight small triangular gussets of balsa wood and glue them to the top and bottom of each rail where it joins the fuselage side.

When you mount the servos to the tray or the rail, you have a chance to isolate them from engine vibration. This is very important, since it will help the servos last a lot longer. You do this by mounting the servos with rubber grommets in the screw holes. All servos come with mounting grommets. Check your radio system instructions for details on using them; but be certain to use them!

Servo Reversing and Control Movement

As you install your servos, turn on the system and check which way the servo rotates. You need to be certain that you connect the pushrod to the side of the servo output arm that will move the control surface in the correct direction: left when the stick is moved left, etc. Suppose you're installing the elevator servo. Connect the elevator pushrod to one side of the servo output arm, and lay the servo in between the mounting rails. Now switch on the system and pull the elevator stick back. Does the elevator go up? If it goes down, you will have to connect the pushrod to the other side of the servo output arm.

If your radio system has servo reversing switches in the transmitter, you don't have to bother with this. Install the servos in the most convenient locations, and connect the pushrods. Turn on the radio and pull the elevator stick back. If the elevator goes down instead of up, move the servo reversing switch for the elevator from one side to the other. Check all other controls for proper direction of servo movement.

Throttle Linkage

You will need to route the throttle pushrod past the fuel tank in most airplanes. It helps to have a very flexible pushrod to do this. In most cases, flexible rods like Sullivan Gold-N-Rods will work fine.

If you need to snake the throttle pushrod through some tight turns, Standale Aircraft Co. makes a product called EZ-Throttle. It's a length of thin nylon tubing with a solid nylon pushrod in the middle. You can literally tie this stuff in a knot and it'll work fine.

One thing that can make throttle connections much easier is the fuel tank itself. Some tanks come with slots molded into the sides so that a pushrod can pass by. Sullivan sells a line of tanks that are made from flexible plastic. These are very easy to install and make installing the throttle pushrod simple.

Aileron Linkages

There are two basic types of aileron linkages. The first uses pushrods that go through the wing structure to a control horn on the aileron. Since the aileron servo is mounted in the middle of the wing, this means the pushrod has to negotiate a 90-degree

Ailerons are usually set up with torque rods for control. These rods run along the center of the wing trailing edge, and project straight down into the fuselage. The aileron servo sits in a pocket in the underside of the wing, and connects to the torque rods with adjustable pushrods. (Photo by Jennifer Pratt)

angle to get to the aileron horn. If you use a flexible pushrod for this, you can use a single piece of pushrod in a curve. If you are using solid pushrods, you'll need some sort of 90-degree bellcrank buried in the wing. If the plans call for the bellcrank setup, bellcranks will be included with the kit hardware.

The other standard aileron linkage is the torque rod. A rod is buried in the trailing edge of the wing from the aileron inboard side to the wing center section. This rod turns freely in a tube. The assembly is in a straight line with the leading edge of the aileron. On the aileron end, a 90-degree hook bent into the end of the rod projects into a hole in the leading edge of the aileron. On the other end, another 90 degree bend projects downward from the underside of the wing. This projection is threaded, and connectors are screwed down onto the threads. The aileron servo rests in the center of the wing, upside down. Connecting rods go from the servo arms to the torque rods on either side.

Of the two, I prefer the torque rod linkage. It's much easier to install, since you flip the wing over and all of the linkages are right there. There's no need for a control horn on the outside of the aileron surface, since the rod projects into a hole in the aileron. And it's much easier to adjust; you can increase the aileron travel by screwing the connectors farther down the projecting threaded ends of the torque rods. Finally, it's easier to get at and replace the servo if necessary.

If you want this kind of linkage and your plane isn't set up for it, you have to plan it before you build the wing. The torque rod tube rests in a slot in the wing trailing edge, and must be parallel with the aileron hinge line. Look at the wing plans and figure out where this needs to go.

Receiver

Once the servos are all mounted, hook them up to the receiver. Your aileron servo won't be connected directly to the receiver; instead, a short extension cord (almost always supplied with your radio system) will plug into the aileron channel plug on the receiver. This allows you to install the receiver and not have to take it out and reinstall it every time you put the wing on the plane.

With all wires connected, ascertain the best spot for mounting the receiver. They are usually placed forward of the servo rails on the floor of the fuselage. Wrap the receiver in a layer of foam rubber, loosely held in place with a rubber band or a length of masking tape. This is critical; without this protection from engine vibration, the best receivers can fail. Now push the receiver down into its spot, and hold it in place by packing more rubber in around it. Unless your plane will go through a lot of violent aerobatics, it usually isn't necessary to do more to keep the receiver from moving around.

Antenna

Last but not least, we're going to look for the proper place to route the receiver antenna. It may seem obvious, but do remember to check that you have done something with the antenna! The first time I bought an ACOMS FM four-channel system, three years ago, I installed it in my old faithful Aeronca Champ. I put three flights on it before I realized that I had never un-coiled the receiver antenna, and it was still resting on top of the receiver under the wing! Now, that's an excellent test of a radio system . . . but I *don't* recommend it! I was very lucky. A receiver antenna that is wrapped back on itself in any way reduces the receiver sensitivity drastically.

When you route the antenna, avoid all other electrical wiring in the plane. Impulses going along those wires can cause interference to the signals being received by the antenna. I like to lead my antennas up the side of the fuselage and out behind the wing, or back through a tube mounted in the fuselage. Short lengths of NyRod or Gold-N-Rod tubing work well for this; I usually use pieces of model rocket launch lugs, since they cut and glue very easily.

Some kits, especially scale models, will provide you with a length of plastic tubing to house the receiver antenna. This tubing is sometimes a very tight fit, and stuffing the antenna through it can be a very frustrating job! I generally replace this tubing with a length of Gold-N-Rod outer tubing. If you're stuck with using the smaller diameter tubing, give it a shot of some spray lubricant, such as WD-40, inside its entire length. Alternatively, dab a little silicon lube on the receiver antenna as you stuff it through.

Once the antenna is outside the fuselage, it needs to be secured somewhere. If you've led it out behind the wing, the usual procedure is to attach it to the top of the vertical fin. This puts it out in the open air and holds it straight, where it is most sensitive to your transmitter signals. You can use several different methods to attach the antenna to the fin, as long as you don't tie the antenna back on itself in any kind of knot. This will reduce sensitivity.

I use a very simple method to attach the receiver antenna to the fin. I drill two very small holes in the fin, and thread the antenna through them. It's all it needs to hold it straight. The holes should be spaced about half an inch apart.

SOME POPULAR TRAINERS REVIEWED

Goldberg Eaglet and Eagle. Since the introduction of the Eaglet 50 and Eagle 63 by Carl Goldberg Models, they've become the most popular trainer planes on the market. There are several reasons for the great success of these planes. They are very well engineered, meaning that none of the construction is beyond the ability of a typical beginner. The prices of the kits are reasonable. They are very flyable planes with no bad habits. Most important, both kits have beautifully drawn plans and outstanding instruction manuals that are illustrated with photos at each step.

When you open up an Eagle box, you'll be presented with carefully sorted stacks of wood. The windshield and windows are molded from clear plastic. The wire landing gear are shaped for you, and there's a bunch of hardware. You need to buy an engine, a fuel tank, an engine mount, and a radio system before you start.

The Eaglet kit mounts the engine on a plywood breakaway plate, which is bolted to hardwood engine bearers that run into the fuselage. This is a very good way of mounting an engine, but it's more work than using a standard plastic or aluminum engine mount. I found it very easy to modify the Eaglet for mounting the engine directly to the firewall; just use a razor saw to slice off the engine bearers flush with the firewall. This would allow you to use the K&B .20 Sportster engine, which comes with its own engine mount designed to bolt to the firewall. Use the same bolts and blind nuts that are included in the

The Eagle is a larger version of the Carl Goldberg Eaglet. Designed for .40 engines, it can be built with or without ailerons. Hundreds of new pilots have learned with an Eagle. (Photo courtesy Carl Goldberg Models)

Eaglet kit for bolting the ply breakaway plate to the bearers to bolt the mount in place through the firewall.

In exactly the same manner, the new K&B .45 Sportster engine would be an excellent choice for the Eagle. The engine puts out more than enough power, and its engine mount will fit easily against the Eagle's firewall. Both K&B Sportster engines are clean, simple, and friendly to beginners. When you add in their prices, which are considerably better than most imported engines of the same size, there's really no better choice.

I recommend building the Eaglet and Eagle in the four-channel versions. It isn't complicated, thanks to the instructions. You've almost certainly bought a four-channel radio anyway, since three-channel radios are not any cheaper than four-channel sets. If you want to simplify the Eaglet, build it without ailerons; it flies very well in this mode. But the ailerons add a dimension of control that you'll enjoy.

While the Eaglet and Eagle are designed to be built and flown by beginners, this doesn't mean they're as easy to build as an almost-ready-to-fly model. These kits are intended to teach, and they do that job very well; building and flying one will give you all the basic knowledge you need to progress in the hobby. You might like to buy an ARF plane to practice with while you're building your Eagle; it'll take away some of the urgency to get the Eagle in the air and help you avoid crashing it.

In fact, there are several products that are intended just for this purpose. One such is the Dura-Plane, an ugly duckling of a trainer plane that is just about crash-proof. The Dura-Plane doesn't fly as well as an Eagle, a Kadet, or a Headmaster, but it flies well, and it will come out of the accidents that all beginners have and still be flyable. I look on ARF planes like the Dura-Plane as kind of a sparring partner; it's a plane you can beat up on while you're getting ready to take on the planes you're building.

SIG Kadet. The classic trainer plane for many years has been the SIG Kadet. This little beauty is available in two versions: with ailerons, or without. Both are fine-flying airplanes with a wide range of different engines. Over more years than I can remember, the Kadet has been the T-38 of RC trainers.

Like all SIG kits, the Kadet has excellent wood and full-size plans. The instructions contain lots of good advice from the SIG Factory Fliers. Building a Kadet will teach you all of the basic techniques for building from plans and working with balsa wood.

The Kadet's flying characteristics are friendly and predictable. It handles well on the ground, and

The SIG Kadet has been a standard trainer plane for many, many years. It's still one of the best. Solid and stable in flight, the kit teaches basic building techniques. (Photo courtesy SIG Manufacturing)

since it requires a touch of up elevator to get into the air, you can practice short hops and fast taxis with it easily.

Last year SIG came out with a giant-sized Kadet, the Kadet Senior. In terms of its flying characteristics, the Kadet Senior is one of the nicest flying planes I've ever seen. It has a huge amount of wing for its weight, so it flies slowly and gently. You can tool it slowly around the sky, getting smoother and smoother as you gain experience. Any inexpensive .40 engine will be more than adequate. A four-stroke, such as the Saito .45, is perfect. Landings are gentle, giving you plenty of time to think of what you're doing. I've never flown a plane that was better for practicing approaches and landings. As the Kadet Senior passes overhead, I understand why some of my friends at SIG refer to the Kadet Senior as "the balsa overcast;" it blots out the sun!

I understand that the SIG folks have been told that the Kadet Senior is just too big to fit in some cars, so they have a "Kadet Seniorita" on the drawing boards. It'll preserve the great flying characteristics of the Senior, but be more convenient to tote around.

Top Flite Elder. If boxy-looking trainer planes just don't appeal to you, but an open-cockpit pre-WWI plane turns you on, you can learn to fly on an Elder from Top Flite Models. There are Elder kits in two different sizes, one for .20 engines and one for .40s. They're both dreamy fliers with all kinds of charm, on the ground and in the the air.

Although I suspect it wasn't really intended to be a trainer, I can heartily recommend either Elder as an excellent first-time kit. The instructions are very good, and the plan is clear and simple. There's plenty of wing on this plane, so you'll have to tape the two plan sections together before you start.

The landing gear requires soldering in a couple of places. This is an easy process as long as the instructions are followed. Wrap the landing gear pieces to be soldered tightly with about four inches of soft copper wire. Now dab a solder flux like Super Safe on the wire. Finally, heat the wire with your soldering iron or gun until the flux sizzles before you touch the solder to it. Touch the solder to the land-

ing gear wire near the soldering iron, not to the tip of the iron. This makes sure that there's enough heat to allow the liquid solder to wick completely through the wires. I suggest giving the completed landing gear a quick shot of black RustOleum or similar spray paint.

The die-cut parts in these kits are very good, with no crushing evident around the cut lines. You should be aware that many pieces are very similar. There are marks on the die-cut sheets near each part that identify the part. You should either punch out the parts only as you need them, or write the part number on each piece with a soft lead pencil.

One nice feature about the way the wing is built is that you build the center section first. This allows you to pin it down flat and attach the two outer sections at the correct dihedral angle. I found this easier than the usual method of pinning one panel flat and propping the other up at the tip.

The fuselage box is built from quarter-inch square balsa and spruce. I recommend the use of a thin-bladed razor saw to get these cuts precisely right. A miter box is very helpful to make the cut ends perfect; you can buy razor saws in sets with a small miter box.

Hooking up the controls is simple, since the rear of the fuselage is open. Control pushrods are provided in the kit. Lightweight wheels, such as the Williams Brothers Vintage wheels, are recommended. The Elders are three-channel taildraggers, which really simplifies the radio installation.

Flying is a delight. There's plenty of rudder for adequate ground handling, even without a steerable tail skid. You should practice your takeoff runs at first, since you'll have to add some rudder as you increase the throttle to keep it straight. The Elder takes off quickly and climbs out well. It also settles in very nicely when the engine is cut to idle, so you don't have to set up a long approach.

Peck-Polymers Prairie Bird. Peck-Polymers is famous for their lovely little rubber-powered scale model kits. They also produce free-flight kits for contest and sport flying. One of their classic FF jobs is the Prairie Bird, a little squarish cabin plane with its wingtips cranked up. It's intended for beginners, since the structure is square and simple.

The Prairie Bird from Peck-Polymers is a lightweight, gentle-flying airplane. It flies so slowly that anyone can fly it with confidence. The fuselage is made of die-cut balsa sheet, and the formers fit in slots in the side. Gas or electric motors can be used; parts are included for either. (Photo by Jennifer Pratt)

I've built several of them, and helped youngsters build more. They always fly until we break the rubber bands!

About a year ago, Bob Peck decided that if the Prairie Bird was a good free-flight model, it'd make a good RC ship. He scaled it up to three times the size of the original, and turned one classic into two. The RC Prairie Bird is one of the friendliest planes I've ever had the pleasure of flying. Actually, you don't really fly the PB; you just make an occasional suggestion.

The Prairie Bird kit is lovely. As with all Peck kits, the wood is selected by hand, and inspected by people who are accustomed to picking good wood for free-flight ships. This is among the finest wood I've seen in a kit box. The fuselage sides are die-cut and slotted; assembling the fuselage box is a matter of fitting the tabs in the sides of the bulkheads into the correct slots in the fuselage. The first thing you should do is mark each piece with a soft lead pencil. Illustrations on the first page of the instructions show you where every part is on each die-cut sheet.

You can build the Prairie Bird for an 05-size electric motor or an .09 to .15 gas motor. The kit in-

cludes two firewalls; you select the one for the power you want to use. The plans show all details of the difference in construction between the gas and electric version. I found the instructions to be lacking in some details, and a beginner will have to study the plans carefully. If you have already built models, you'll have no problems at all.

I installed a PAW .049 Diesel in my Prairie Bird, just to be different. It was less power than the kit calls for. On the first flight, which was only the second time the little PAW had been run, I had no trouble hand-launching the plane, but it was distinctly underpowered. Still, the PB caught a light thermal and spiraled up to a good altitude, then cruised around happily when the engine quit. I refueled it, leaned the engine out a little more, and launched again. This time we got right up to altitude and were doing wide, lazy circles in no time at all.

I'm going to put a PAW .09 in the Prairie Bird soon. The .049 flies it very well, but it takes full throttle through the whole flight. The PAW throttles beautifully, so it's going in a smaller plane where it can show its stuff.

Coverite Black Baron Trainer. Another trainer kit that doesn't look like a flying box is the

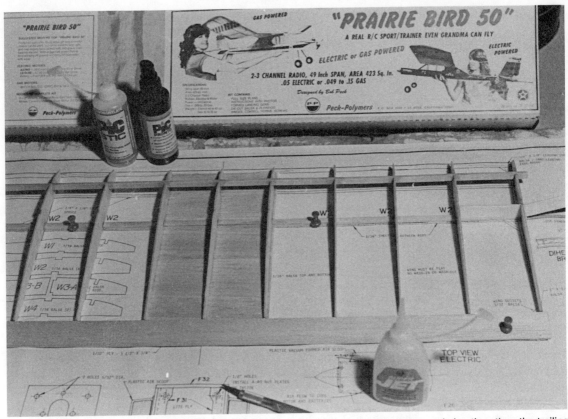

The Prairie Bird wing structure is conventional. Die-cut ribs are glued over bottom spars and sheeting, then the trailing edge and top spar are attached. (Photo by Jennifer Pratt)

Black Baron Special Trainer from Coverite. This classy-looking ship is designed for four channels, so flying takes a bit more skill than a three-channel floater. You can build the BB Special as a taildragger or with tricycle gear. A very well-written instruction manual spells everything out well, including covering and finishing. A rank beginner can put the BB Special together with little or no help and show up at the field with a fine-flying plane.

The wood quality is very good, with fine die-cutting. All the plastic pieces are trimmed for you except the covering of the wing center section, which is very simple. The fuselage is a crutch structure with sheet sides drawn together at the rear. You really have to work at it to get it wrong. A plastic piece fits over the entire rear of the fuselage box, all the way out to the tail. CyA glue works very well

for attaching this kind of molded plastic to the wooden fuselage. The plastic is sandable, so the joint can be made to almost disappear.

The engine is covered with a neat plastic cowl; you cut away sections of the front of the cowl to clear the exhaust of whatever engine you install. A .40 two-stroke engine is recommended; since the plane comes out to about 4 ½ pounds, that's adequate power. A .45 or .46 four-stroke would also be an excellent choice for power.

The wing panels are joined by a long dihedral brace made from ⅛ plywood. This prevents misalignment and makes for a very strong wing.

The Black Baron Special flies with no surprises. I enjoy taildraggers, but you may want to build the optional nosewheel. One of the nicest flying characteristics of the BB Special is the way it flies at low

The Black Baron Trainer from Coverite is a sleek-looking machine that is really easy to build. The fuselage top is a plastic piece that fits over the wooden fuselage sides. The BB Trainer can be built for taildragger or tricycle landing gear. (Photo courtesy Coverite)

airspeeds. The ailerons remain effective right up to the point of a stall. Approaches can be made nose-high with plenty of control.

Ace Air Scout. The Ace Air Scout has been around for a lot of years, but never achieved the following it deserves. I really don't know why; it's a delightful plane. It's easy to assemble, durable, and good looking. Why have so few of us noticed it?

The Air Scout kit comes with a very nice set of instructions, but no full-size plan. Instead, there's a half-size assembly drawing. There's really no need for a big plan, since the die-cut parts assemble so well. The fuselage is mostly die-cut light ply, which cuts very cleanly. The pieces slot together and are self-jigging; it's easy to get them straight.

I particularly like the wing attachment system on the Air Scout. Instead of using rubber bands, you're given two nylon bolts and flanged nylon nuts. The nuts glue into holes in two hardwood pieces mounted inside the fuselage under the rear of the wing. The bolts go down through holes in the wing, and thread into these nuts—neat and simple! Usually, when using nylon bolts, you have to thread the holes in the wing hold-down blocks. This system is much easier.

The Air Scout is a three-channel plane, with plenty of dihedral in the wing. A .20-.25 two-stroke engine is plenty of power. I installed a Saito .30 four-stroke, a delightful engine that I'd had on several other planes. It was a happy marriage. The Saito pulled the Air Scout smartly off the grass on take-off, and flew it very well at half throttle. The Air Scout is small enough to hand-launch very easily.

After three years, two close encounters with trees, one fast taxi into the side of a car, and several cartwheel landings, the Air Scout is still helping people learn to fly at my field. I can hand the plane to just about anyone with confidence. I expect a few more years of service from this perky plane—after which, I'll probably build another one!

ARF: ALMOST READY TO FLY

Almost Ready to Fly (ARF) planes are often a good way to start flying RC. They are easy for an inexperienced builder to put together. They come out straight and flyable if you follow the instructions. And they let you get right into flying, while you're improving your building skills on your second airplane.

Many almost-ready-to-fly planes come built and covered, needing only to be assembled. The E-Z kits are available from Hobby Shack; about four hours of work will put them in the air. (Photo by Jennifer Pratt)

On the negative side, ARF planes are more expensive than kits. They do a lot of the building for you, and labor is expensive. ARF kits are often heavier than a kit plane of the same size, so they require bigger engines and fly faster. Sometimes they can be hard to repair. You might find yourself having to replace parts instead of fixing them. Finally, there is no real definition of "ready to fly." Some kits that are called ARFs can be built by a beginner in hours; others will take an expert builder a week.

Your hobby dealer can save you a lot of money here. He knows his products, and will steer you right. After all, he wants you for a steady customer . . . that won't happen if he gives you bad advice!

The Super Box Fly planes from Hobby Shack come with a flashy color pattern painted on. All you have to do is join the wings, attach the tail, install the engine and radio, and you're ready. (Photo courtesy *Model Retailer* magazine)

John Elliott of Cox Hobbies shows off their newest RC trainer, the PT-19. It comes virtually ready to go, with an .049 engine installed. Put in a two-channel radio, rubber band the wing on, and fly! (Photo courtesy *Model Retailer* magazine)

I've built and flown many ARF kits. There are more introduced all the time, so I can't hope to give you a complete list. I'll try to give an overview, though, so you'll recognize the types of ARFs and know what to expect.

MRC Foam Planes. MRC has three ARF airplanes. All are molded from thick foam, and come with the appropriate Enya engine and tank already installed, the pushrods in place, and the steerable nosewheel connected. This is a real time- and sweat-saver. I find the foam construction excellent, because when you crash and break it, you get big pieces that are easy to epoxy back together.

The Trainer Hawk is a trainer plane intended for the beginner. It uses three channels for control: rudder, elevator and throttle. The nosewheel is steerable, so ground handling is very good. An Enya .15 engine comes installed in the fuselage. You will spend about three hours epoxying the tail on the plane, putting on the self-adhesive decals, and fitting the receiver, battery, and servos into the pockets molded inside the fuselage. The Trainer Hawk is a docile plane that will get off the ground fast and then fly very slowly at half throttle. It's also a rugged little devil. I've seen them strained through trees, broken in half, and spiraled straight in, and all were flying again as soon as the epoxy set. The Enya engine is a real beauty, and will far outlive the airplane; when you finally get tired of the Hawk, the engine would go beautifully in a Goldberg Eaglet 50 or similar small trainer.

The MRC Skyhawk is a semi-scale Cessna Skyhawk molded entirely out of foam. It's big! I flew one of the first ones that was produced, and after the people at MRC read my report on the plane they started affectionately referring to the Skyhawk as

MRC's all-foam Trainer Hawk is a very popular beginner plane. It comes with an Enya .15 engine already installed. The radio receiver, battery and servos fit into molded pockets inside the fuselage. It's a tough little plane that performs well. (Photo courtesy *Model Retailer* magazine)

"Fat Albert." The fuselage looks as if you could store a cold six-pack in it. You won't have any trouble getting your hands inside to install the radio!

You will spend a little more time building the Skyhawk than you would on the Trainer Hawk described above. The hard work is done: The engine is installed, and the steerable nosegear and pushrods for the tail surfaces are rigged. The wing comes in two panels that have to be joined, and the servo that controls the ailerons has to be installed. The aileron pushrods are in place, and all the control surfaces are hinged.

The Skyhawk's Enya .35 engine seems awfully small in the nose of that big, boxy fuselage, but it has all the power you need. It's fitted with an oversize prop. It's important to break in the engine by running it on the ground, as described in the instructions. This gives you a chance to get familiar with the engine as well as getting it tuned up to give you the maximum power output.

Flying the Skyhawk is a delight. It lumbers happily around the sky, with smooth, slow responses to all controls. I've never seen a better aileron trainer.

MRC's Cherokee is a foam plane like the Trainer Hawk and Cessna, but ailerons are optional. The Cherokee's construction is very similar to the others, and won't take any longer to put together.

It's a low-wing airplane, which means that it isn't quite as stable as the other two; but it's still perfectly flyable by a beginner. I recommend going ahead and installing the ailerons.

MRC also sells a couple of electric-powered foam airplanes. While they are excellent planes, I don't really recommend them as your first plane. They are not as easy to fly as the gas-powered models, and will not fly as long. You want long flights while you're learning, to help you build your experience (and confidence!).

RPM. You'll find several ready-to-fly airplanes by RPM in your local hobby shop. They are excellent, with good construction, adequate instructions, and very good flying ability. I've built two, the electric-powered Snark 5T and the Cherokee. Both went together very quickly—one evening for the Snark and two for the Cherokee.

The Cherokee wing is joined by a main spar laminated from a piece of balsa and a piece of ply, and a rear brace of ply. The dowel that holds the front of the wing in place goes into a precut rib piece that you glue to the front of one wing half; 30-minute epoxy is supplied with the kit, so you have plenty of time to get this right.

The only thing I found even slightly difficult about attaching the wing came when it was time to drill it for the hold-down bolts. The mounting blocks

There aren't many parts to the MRC Trainer Hawk. All it takes to assemble it is some epoxy and a few hours of time. (Photo by Jennifer Pratt)

are already mounted in the fuselage, and blind nuts are mounted in the holes. When you put on the wing, you cover those holes. You have to drill through the wing and hit them. I drew light guide lines on the back of the fuselage and on the wing to give me the approximate location. Then I poked a T-pin through where I thought the hole was. I hit 'em both on the second try, and had no problem drilling through with Ace Handrills. The kit includes rubber O-rings to slip over the bolts to keep them in place in the wing—a thoughtful touch.

The Cherokee includes a large fuel tank that fits into holes in the formers behind the firewall. Brackets for the nosewheel are molded into the aluminum motor mount, which comes mounted on the firewall. You just slip the nose gear into the brackets and secure it with collars. The arms of the engine mount are cut away on top to the thickness of the

mounting lugs on the engine you'll use. To mount an engine, you attach a mounting pad to each engine mounting lug. The mounting pad is a thin strip of steel with two elongated holes in the ends. These holes will allow you to bolt the mounting pad, with the engine attached, to the arms of the engine mount. The mount is wide to accommodate .60-.80 size four-stroke engines, so there are two sets of mounting pads: a narrow set for four-strokes, and a wide set for two-strokes.

The tail surfaces are already built. They mount with epoxy; first the stabilizer, then the vertical fin, then the fairing that covers the rear of the fuselage. After cutting slots in the fairing to clear the rudder pushrod, the rudder hinges are epoxied in place.

There's plenty of room inside the fuselage for easy radio installation. A plywood servo tray fits most standard servos and epoxies in place between two fuselage formers. The pushrods are already made and fit easily into the fuselage. The control horns that bolt to the rudder and elevator have copper tubes that sheath the bolts where they go through the surfaces, so you can't crush the surface by overtightening the bolts.

The Cherokee is lively with a four-stroke .60. I installed an Enya, and the performance was all I could wish. It flies inverted with slight forward pressure on the elevator stick. I don't consider the Cherokee gentle enough for a first airplane, but it'll be a fine second model or proficiency plane for practicing your aerobatics.

Polk's Hobbies. Polk's Model Craft Hobbies is producing several ready-to-fly airplane kits. They are all of built-up construction rather than solid foam, and are very well built and quite lightweight.

I had a look at one of Polk's RTFs, the Challenger 25, at a recent trade show. It's a conventional-looking trainer plane. The eye-opening part of the kit isn't the plane itself, it's what else is in the box: an engine installed in the fuselage, and a complete four-channel radio system with receiver and servos installed where they belong. Now, that's coming closer to the concept of ready-to-fly than just about anything else I've seen. All you have to do is join the wing halves, bolt on the landing gear and muffler, glue the tail on and connect the pushrods, put batteries in the radio system, and go.

There are two Challengers in the Polk ARF line, one with a .25 engine installed, and one with a .40. Other Polk ARFs include the Satellite 40, a .40 size high-wing trainer; the Sharp 45, a sport pattern airplane; and the Swan, a neat little glider.

The Polk ARFs that include engines come with Blue Bird engines, made in Taiwan. These are nice little engines—not spectacular performers, but friendly. I value ease of handling above power output in this kind of plane. I've run their .25 and I like it; it broke in quickly and has been easy to start. Like many engines that come with RTF airplanes, the engine will probably outlive the plane.

Lanier. Lanier RC has been cranking out a unique line of RTF kits for a lot of years. These are tough, strong, durable planes made from plastic and foam. A typical Lanier fuselage has a wood skeleton with two plastic halves glued to it; the wings are foam, skinned with high-impact plastic sheet. This

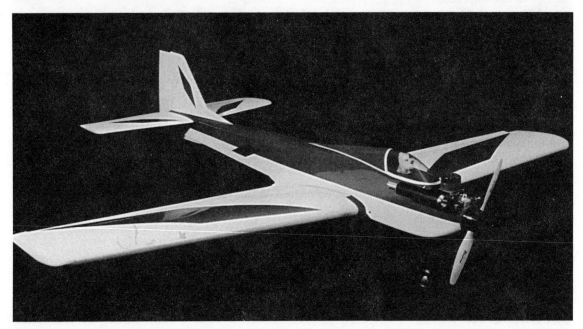

Lanier RC makes a large line of almost-ready-to-fly models that are hot performers. The fuselage is molded plastic, formed over a hardwood crutch. The wings are foam, sheeted with plastic. (Photo courtesy *Model Retailer* magazine)

is a good way to produce airplanes. Buying a Lanier plane saves you from having to do any major construction.

These kits are available in a wide range, suitable for different skill levels. If you're a beginner, look for flat-bottom airfoils and three channels of control, like the Pinto, Sky Scooter, or Cessna. Intermediate trainers have symmetrical airfoils and ailerons, like the Comet and Transit. For experienced fliers, Lanier offers several hot Sport Aerobatics planes like the P-51, Caprice, and Jester. There's even a biplane, the Rebel, with sport aerobatics capability. You can even order them in different colors.

Lanier kits do involve a good deal of work to assemble—more than most other RTF airplanes. You'll need some hardware: a fuel tank and tubing, engine mounting bolts, hinges, control horns, and wheels. The motor mounts to hardwood rails in the engine compartment. You can use machine screws to attach the engine, or bolts threaded into blind nuts; I have been perfectly happy with machine screws, which are a lot easier to install. The servos mount on hardwood rails, which glue to the crutch sides. There's plenty of room in all of the Lanier kits to put in any kind of radio. Wing halves are joined with epoxy and plywood joiners; the dihedral angle is preset and impossible to get wrong. Sheets of the same plastic that is laminated over the wing fit over the wing joints.

Indy RC. Indy RC imports the MK line of ready-to-fly model kits. These are also available from World Engines, and are sold extensively in hobby shops at the same prices (or slightly better) than you can buy them through mail order. MK kits are very well constructed and quite easy to put together.

Indy also imports their own line of RTF kits. These are made by Lion Models and are very similar to the MK and Polk kits. There is quite a range of these kits, from sport models to aerobatic jobs. A standout is their Laser, done up in Bud Light regalia, as flown by full-scale aerobatics pilot Leo Loudenslager. It's a real stormer in the hands of a good pilot, with a .90 four-stroke or .60 two-stroke engine.

Indy's Christen Eagle is another remarkable

RTF. The color pattern is outstanding; it's applied at the factory as part of the skinning going over the balsa skeleton. It's a big plane, intended for .90 two-stroke or 1.20 four-stroke engines. This is not a trainer plane, however; it flies like the prototype, and needs a skilled hand at the controls.

Dura Craft. A brand new product appeared on the RTF trainer scene this year. It's called the Dura-Plane, and the name sums it up well. It's not designed to win any beauty contests; while it may not be the ugliest plane I've ever seen, it's definitely in the top five. The beauty of the Dura-Plane shows up when you try to destroy it. This is as close to an indestructible airplane as I've ever seen.

The Dura-Plane was created by an RC flier who remembered the frustration he felt after his first crash. A beginner puts a lot of work into his first plane, when everything is new to him. Even if he builds it straight and has expert help in learning to fly, that plane is going to crash sooner or later. The experience can be devastating, but crashing is part of learning and you can't avoid it. So why not provide a beginner with a plane that, when it crashes, can be quickly and easily rebuilt? It doesn't have to be his pride and joy; it just has to be something for him to do his crashing on while he learns.

The Dura-Plane consists of a rectangular plastic box, open on the ends. An aluminum channel bolts into the bottom of the box and sticks out one end. The tail surfaces, which are made of ¼-inch balsa, bolt to the far end of the channel. The channel is just wide enough to take a standard servo; you jam the three servos into it, the throttle servo in front. Flexible pushrods for the elevator and rudder are clipped to the channel. The servos fit into the end of the channel inside the plastic box. Right ahead of the servos, you install your receiver battery, wrapped in foam. The firewall bolts to the front end of the box; a hole in it allows the throttle pushrod to come through. The engine bolts to the firewall, and stays right out in the open where you can work on it. The aluminum landing gear is bolted to the bottom of the box with nylon bolts. The wing is foam and is held in place with rubber bands that go around hooks in the sides of the box.

It's hard to imagine anything simpler than the

Chip Smith holds a DuraPlane, a new trainer kit. The DuraPlane is tough enough to take the hardest crashes. It isn't unbreakable, but everything on it is quickly and inexpensively replaceable.

Dura-Plane. Everything is easy to reach for adjustment and repair. If you need to work on the radio, you disconnect the throttle pushrod and unbolt the aluminum channel from the bottom of the box; the whole business comes out the back. The receiver is wrapped in foam and jammed in the rear of the box, out of harm's way.

In a crash, what's going to break? The plastic box won't crack unless it's a really cold day. The aluminum channel won't bend, and if the tail surfaces should get broken, they're easily fixed or replaced. If the foam wing breaks, a little five-minute epoxy will have it back together. If the landing gear takes a really hard landing, the nylon bolts break away and you have to reattach the gear with two new ones. They're a standard size sold in hobby shops and

hardware stores.

The engine is exposed, right up there in the front. In a crash, you'll probably break a prop. In a bad crash, you could break off the needle valve or muffler. In a *really* bad crash, the engine mount will snap. Doing serious damage to the engine is unlikely.

The Dura-Plane folks recommend the K&B .20 Sportster engine. It's a beautiful engine, as friendly as any I've ever played with; it's easy to break in and adjust. For the crasher, its true beauty will come from the fact that it's made in the U.S. Parts are plentiful and cheap. If you snap off the needle valve, a whole new carburetor is only a few bucks. Likewise the muffler stack. The neat little backplate engine mount that comes with the K&B .20 is less than

$5 to replace. And if you somehow manage to "land" straight down on a slab of granite, you can go to just about any hobby shop and buy a whole new engine for less than $40.

I'm really impressed with this kit. Any beginner should have no difficulty putting it together, and it's very easy to fly. When you realize that it is extending the lifespans of prettier all-wood airplanes, the tough, ugly little Dura-Plane looks better all the time.

Chapter 5

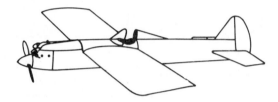

Covering and Finishing

THERE ARE MANY METHODS OF COVERING AND FINishing your model. Which one you select depends on the model and on your personal preference. As you try different finishing techniques, you'll develop your own routines and methods for getting the best finish. Before long you'll find what works best for you.

IRON-ON COVERINGS

Most sport modelers use a one-step iron-on covering. These are inexpensive and convenient, and they give a tough finish with minimal effort. Several brands are available with slightly different characteristics for different situations.

MonoKote. The first of these to be introduced was MonoKote. MonoKote is a plastic film available in a wide range of colors. It's very easy to work with. MonoKote has become the standard method for covering planes. In fact, even though ''MonoKote'' is a registered trademark, you'll hear people using it as a verb: "I *MonoKoted* my wing yesterday.''

Coverite. Coverite makes several covering products. Super Coverite is a polyester fabric with an iron-on adhesive. Since it's woven, it stretches and shrinks around corners and curves very easily. It's very lightweight and tough. Permagloss Coverite is cloth with several coats of paint applied. It looks like the doped fabric that used to be used to cover full-size airplanes. For models of ''ragwing'' planes, there's nothing better. Black Baron Film is a plastic film that's very stretchable. The adhesive activates at low temperatures, so Black Baron Film is very good for bare foam. Finally, Micafilm is a unique covering material that has no adhesive on either side. You paint the adhesive onto the structure. Micafilm is very tough, and adds a great deal of torsional strength to an open structure.

Other films. Several companies have introduced other brands of covering film over the last few years. I haven't tried them all, and so can't make specific recommendations. I've heard very good things about ColorTex from Carl Goldberg Models, and one of my friends was very impressed by Goldberg's new Ultrakote. SIG's Supercoat film has been getting good reviews. Try a few of these and find your own favorites.

Applying Iron-On Coverings

It may sound obvious, but the most important rule I've discovered for using iron-on coverings is: *Read the instructions!* I've heard many modelers griping about one covering or another that didn't go on the way they expected. It always turns out that they've always used one brand of covering and gotten accustomed to it. They try another brand, using the same methods as with their traditional covering, and wonder why it doesn't work right! It's an easy trap to fall into.

Why read the instructions? True, many of the basic techniques are the same no matter what brand you're using. This is especially true with films that have a wide range of working temperature, such as MonoKote and Black Baron Film. But most films have a very specific temperature where they go on the easiest and work the best.

Working Temperature of the Covering

Working temperature is important for two reasons: adhesive grab and shrink. The instructions will tell you the best iron temperature for the adhesive to form a solid bond with the airplane surface. If you set your iron too cool, the adhesive may stick, but it will never get the really solid bond it needs to keep fuel and oil from creeping in under the edges. If your iron is set too hot, then the covering can begin to shrink and pull away from the surface before the adhesive has cooled enough to grab properly. It's amazing how many of my friends have reported having all kinds of grief with a certain covering, then gone back and checked the iron temperature and found the reason!

A thermometer also is an essential piece of equipment. An ordinary meat thermometer will work well enough, but the temperature probe won't rest on the iron shoe easily. I use a Pocket Thermometer sold by Coverite. Its coil rests right on the shoe, and you have an accurate temperature reading in under a minute. I've also seen people use the oven thermometers that you stick on the oven wall; just remove the metal case to expose the thermometer element, and rest it on the iron shoe.

The Iron

As for the iron itself, I recommend buying a seal-

A sealing iron is an essential tool if you plan to cover your model with an iron-on film. These have adjustable temperatures for different films. Keep the iron shoe clean and free of scratches. (Photo courtesy *Model Retailer* magazine)

Before you start to cover, turn on your iron and check the temperature. This thermometer is sold by Coverite for this purpose. Check the instructions of the covering film to see what temperature is recommended. (Photo by Jennifer Pratt)

ing iron specifically designed for model covering. You can get away with using a small travel iron, but the model iron will be much more convenient, especially for getting into tight corners. Top Flite sells an excellent iron. It has a replaceable Teflon-coated shoe, which means you don't have to buy a whole new iron when the old one gets scratched up. Top Flite also sells a tool called a Trim Iron, which looks like a soldering iron with a tiny triangular shoe at the tip. This is the greatest for sticking down hard-to-reach spots, such as underneath the stabilizer or around a pushrod exit.

Surface Preparation

Any covering method works best if the surface is properly prepared. This is especially important with an iron-on covering, which is held tight to the surface and is too thin to hide imperfections.

The most important factor in any finish is good

old faithful sandpaper. You used coarse sandpaper to shape the parts and smooth the joints between parts; now grab some fine paper for the *real* work!

See Chapter 2, Your Workshop, for a discussion of different sanding methods and tools. A sanding block is essential for open frameworks and flat-sheeted surfaces. In fact, you should either have several sanding blocks with different grades of sandpaper, or a tool such as the Wedge Lock sanding block that allows you to slip sanding belts on and off the block. For curved surfaces, you need a flexible pad. I've experimented with sponge-type sanding tools which consist of a fairly flexible sanding pad that resembles a cellulose sponge laminated with grit. They work quite well for larger jobs with coarse or medium grit, and are useful for spots you can't reach with a sanding block.

For smoothing and finishing, I prefer a strip of sandpaper folded into thirds. I cut a new sheet of sandpaper into three strips of equal width. Then I fold it over on itself twice. When one surface wears thin, turn the pad over. Then refold it when necessary to expose the third surface. This gives you a grit surface for your fingers, which keeps the pad from slipping as you work.

You'll sometimes run into problems at the joints where two pieces of wood have been glued together. The glue is harder than the surrounding wood, and when you sand it, you remove wood on either side of the glue faster than you remove the glue. Some of the traditional glues such as Ambroid and Titebond don't have this problem, which is why lots of people still use them. But the modern cyanoacrylate (CyA) glues can give you fits when you're trying to smooth things out. This is most noticeable with surfaces that are sheeted or planked with thin balsa.

I've found a solution that works very well. You need a wet-or-dry grade of sandpaper, and one of the super glue solvents such as Z-7 Debonder or Jet De-Solv. Nitromethane-based debonders don't work as well for this, since they evaporate too quickly. Moisten your sanding pad with a squirt of debonder, and go to work on the ridge of glue. A few strokes should smooth it right out. This should be the last step in smoothing the sheeted surface, since the ridges won't show until you've worked over the surrounding wood.

Use a sanding block to fine-sand all open structure, such as the tops of wing ribs and the sides of the fuselage. Look for ridges and blobs of glue at joints in the open structure, and wet-sand with debonder to smooth them out. They'll show up later if you don't deal with them now! I've discovered lumps of glue that actually poked a hole in the covering when I tried to iron it down. The bottom of the wing is a good place to find these, since glue will run down the joints and set against the wax paper on your building board.

So now you've got a smooth structure, with no lumps and ridges. Don't heat up the iron yet! You *could* proceed to iron down a film covering at this point, and it would look okay, but it wouldn't be attached as well as it could be. Sooner or later it'll start to bubble or come up around the edges. A little extra care at this point will pay off in the long run.

All wood absorbs moisture. Balsa wood is more spongelike than most, since it's composed of a lattice-like structure. You need to get some of this moisture out of the wood before you seal it with your covering.

The best way I've found is to poke the wood full of pinholes. You don't need to go all the way through, just enough to make holes in the surface. I know that this is going to make your beautiful smooth surface look like it has a rash, but trust me a little longer!

You can fabricate a tool to make this surface ventilation easier by driving pins through a small block of hard balsa until they come out the other side, then securing the pins with thin super glue. Or you can save yourself some time and effort and buy a tool called a Prep Tacker. Craft-Air makes it, and it costs less than $10. It consists of a thick strip of curved plastic with holes molded in. You push the included map tacks through the holes so the points come out the other side. Then you slip the plastic strip into a sturdy molded handle that secures the map tacks in place. It looks like a Medieval torture device, but it does a great job.

After thoroughly ventilating the structure, I like to leave it overnight to let the moisture escape. If it's summer, this is a very good excuse to turn on your air conditioner.

The next step is to get all the dust from sanding off the surface. Many modelers like to use a painter's tack rag for this. The tack rag is a cloth that has been impregnated with a slightly sticky chemical. Wiping the surface with the tack rag picks up the dust. When the rag isn't tacky any more, you throw it out and get a new one.

I prefer to use a small vacuum cleaner. I inherited our old cannister vac when my wife bought a new one, and it does the job beautifully. It lives under the workbench, with the hose in a large hook at the corner of the bench where it's out of the way. I use the small long-bristle brush on the end of the hose. A thorough vacuuming will leave the structure as dust-free as a tack rag would. The crevice attachment is handy for getting dust and shavings out of corners, too.

If I'm going to use an iron-on covering, I like to use Balsarite as the last step before ironing the covering down. Balsarite seals the surface, which will keep the air that's still trapped inside the wood from coming up and causing bubbles. It also helps the adhesive on the covering grab much faster. I use Balsarite no matter what brand of covering I'm applying to the structure. In fact, the only time I don't use it is when the surface is going to be painted.

Once the Balsarite is painted on, the covering can be applied, reheated, lifted, and reapplied several times without needing more Balsarite. This is even true with Micafilm, which has no adhesive of its own but sticks only where you've put Balsarite.

Balsarite takes about 15 minutes to dry in normal temperature and humidity. When it's dry, you may notice that your beautiful smooth surface isn't quite so smooth any more. Don't worry about it. The heat of the iron will melt the surface of the Balsarite and smooth it down.

Basic Covering Technique

Now, at last, you're ready to do some covering. You'll be dealing with two different surfaces as you work: open structure, such as wings and open fuselage sides; and solid surfaces, such as sheet fu-

Micafilm doesn't have adhesive on it. You adhere it to the framework by painting Balsarite on the surface first. This means the Micafilm sticks only where you want it to. You also save weight, since there's no adhesive between the ribs. (Photo by Jennifer Pratt)

selage sides. The methods used to cover these are completely different from one another, since we require different things from the covering material for each type of surface. On an open framework, we want good adhesion around the edges of the structure, then an even shrink rate to bring the covering up tight between the ribs. On the solid sheet surface, we need as little shrinking as possible to avoid pulling away from the surface as the covering cools and trapping air bubbles which show up later.

Covering Open Frameworks

You should cover the bottom of a wing panel first, so you can curl the edges of the top covering under the edges of the wing panel, where they won't be seen.

My favorite technique for covering wings and other open frameworks comes from Henry Haffke, well-known builder of scale Gee Bee models. Henry works for Coverite, so he might be accused of favoring their covering products, but he's used just about everything on the market at one time or another in the course of a long and successful scale building career.

Henry begins by cutting a piece of covering material that will overlap the edges of the structure to be covered by at least ¼ inch all around.

With his iron set at the right temperature for the adhesive to activate, but not so high as to cause

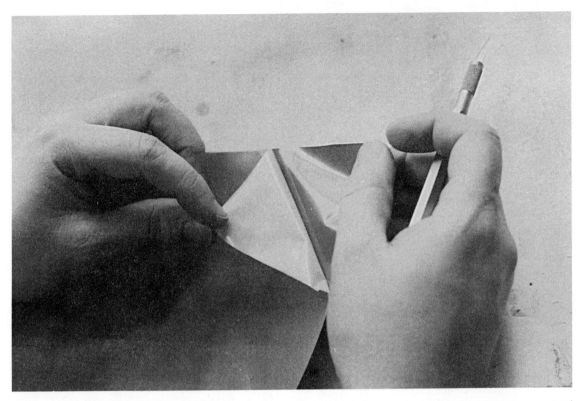

Plastic films come with a backing sheet to protect the adhesive. Measure and cut the covering to size before you peel this backing sheet away. (Photo by Jennifer Pratt)

the material to shrink, Henry tacks down one corner of the material at the wingtip. Then he tacks down the corner diagonally opposite, pulling the covering a bit so that it's smooth. He repeats this process with the other two corners. Sometimes it's necessary to take up one of the corners to pull wrinkles out of the material. It's all right to leave some small wrinkles in, but you should work out as many as you can now rather then depending on the covering to shrink them all out.

With all four corners secured, Henry works his way down one side of the structure, maintaining a little pull to keep it smooth. Then he moves to the opposite side. Now that there's a tightly-adhered side to pull against, Henry really works out most of the wrinkles at this point by pulling the material as hard as necessary. Working along the other two edges in the same way results in a smooth surface without even beginning to shrink the material. This

way, the full shrinking ability of the material is there if you need it.

Henry works slowly, pressing his iron down with a rolling motion and lifting it, rather than rubbing it along the surface of the covering. This gives you a much better bond, and keeps you from scratching the covering if you have a rough spot on your iron shoe.

Covering Solid Surfaces

When you cover a solid surface, such as a solid fuselage side or a sheeted wing, the main problem is to get complete adhesion evenly across the entire surface. The shrinking ability of the covering is not helpful here. The temperature of your iron is crucial. If it's too cool, the adhesive won't get a chance to grab properly. If the iron is too hot, the covering will shrink and can pull completely away from the surface before the adhesive has cooled

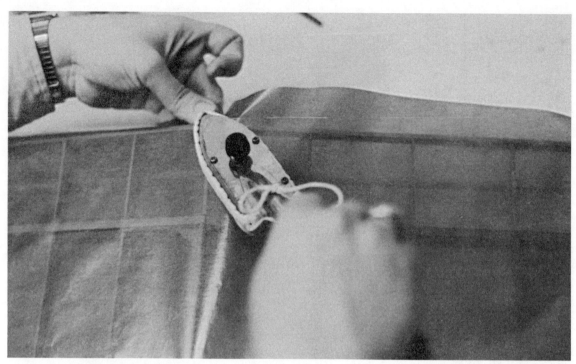

To cover a panel of open framework, start with the corners. Stick each corner down, keeping the covering as smooth as possible. (Photo by Jennifer Pratt)

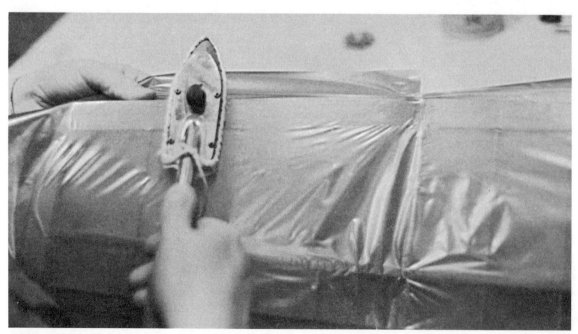

Once the leading edge is attached, do the trailing edge, pulling out wrinkles as you go. When the trailing edge is down, do the sides. Then you can run the iron over the middle, shrinking out any wrinkles that got in. (Photo by Jennifer Pratt)

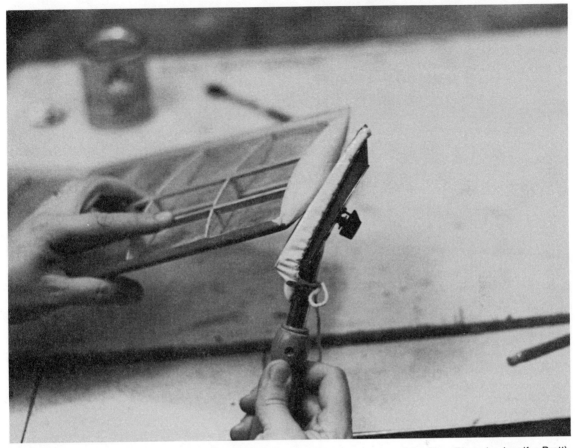

Finally, using a gentle rolling motion with the iron, stick down the trimmed edge of the film. (Photo by Jennifer Pratt)

down enough to grab. Check the instructions for the film you are using, and use a thermometer to get the iron temperature as close as you can to what they recommend.

I like to cover the top and bottom of a fuselage first. This way the seams are underneath and on top of the plane when the sides are covered, where they're less noticeable.

I cover solid surfaces with a technique that is the opposite of the one described above for open structures: I work from the center out. After cutting a piece of covering that will overlap the surface by at least ¼ inch all around, I position it and tack a spot in the center. Then I check to make sure the whole piece is in the position I want it. I learned this one the hard way—by winding up short on one side a few times!

Once you've performed this check, start to work outward from your center spot. Rest the iron on the covering, pressing gently and turning it slightly. Don't press too hard, or you run the risk of scratching the surface with your iron. A cloth pad on your iron is helpful; you can even cover the shoe with a thin cotton sock. You'll probably have to turn up the temperature if you do this; measure the temperature from the surface of the cloth pad.

Once you reach an edge, work the covering around the edge with light pressure. Make sure you do it smoothly, starting from the center of the edge and sealing it completely. If the edge is curved, such as a wing saddle, you will have to cut small vertical slits in the covering to help it conform to the curve. Adhere the covering completely over the edge and down the other side.

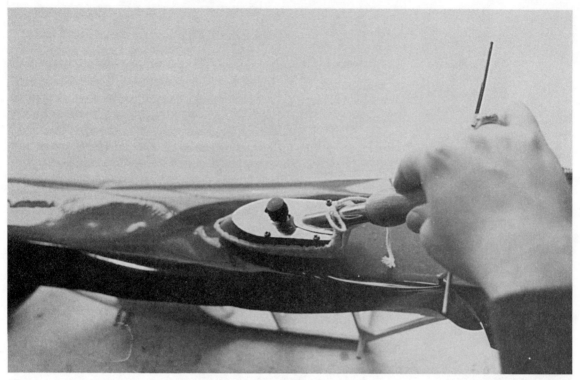

When covering fuselages, cover the top and bottom, then the sides. This puts the seams on the underside and the top when you overlap the side pieces. They're less noticeable there. This is Black Baron Film, which conceals seams very well. (Photo by Jennifer Pratt)

Corners and Curves

One of the most difficult parts to cover is the wingtip, since it is usually a compound curve and the covering has to stretch in one place and shrink in another. Turn your iron up slightly to the temperature recommended for shrinking the covering you're working with. Working from the leading edge of the wing, grasp the covering material and pull it down. Roll your iron shoe over the part that looks the smoothest when you pull it. Work slowly from the front to the back, exerting steady downward pressure on the material. Remember to *roll* your iron; don't *rub* with it. Do a small piece at a time, and it will shrink or stretch smoothly. You should have no wrinkles in the wingtip by the time you finish.

Cleaning the Iron

Irons tend to get gummy after a little use, since some adhesive will ooze out from under the edge of the covering. Sometimes some of the pigment will come out with it and stick to the iron shoe, usually coming off as you start to seal down another color of covering. So check the iron shoe regularly as you work and keep it clean. Coverite sells a product called Ironex for this. I keep a cloth pad moist with Ironex handy as I work. It's simple to just occasionally wipe the iron shoe on the cloth when it needs it. The Ironex also works great for cleaning up little streaks of adhesive or pigment that can ooze out around the edges and seams of the covering. It'll take the streaks right up without loosening the edge of the covering.

I mentioned before that occasionally it's a good idea to use a thin cloth pad between the iron and the covering. A piece of cotton or muslin works fine for this, and can be washed or tossed out when it gets dirty. A thin cotton sock can do the same job, and has the advantage of staying with the iron as

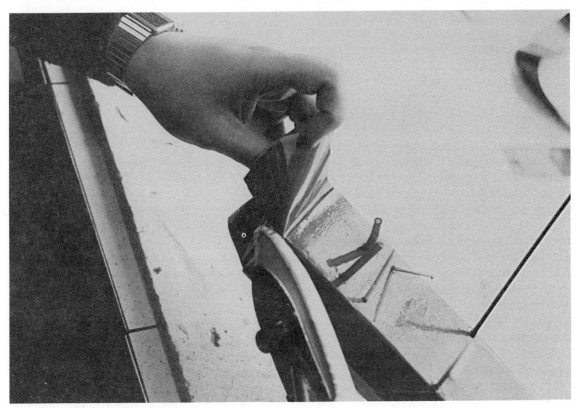

To work the film around corners, hold the end firmly and roll the iron around the corner. The heated film will stretch without much pressure. Slit the film at the corners and work it down flat. (Photo by Jennifer Pratt)

you move it. Buy a child-size sock and use rubber bands around the handle (not the shoe!) of the iron to hold it in place.

I've used a product called a Hot Sock that I bought at a trade show one year. It's a little cotton bag with a drawstring. It fits around the base of the iron, and the drawstring holds it in place. Top Flite, the MonoKote people, sell the Hot Sock; your local hobby shop will almost certainly have them. With a Hot Sock on your iron, you can't possibly scratch the covering material, and color that bleeds onto the iron won't smear around.

PAINTING

If you can't find a color of iron-on covering that you want, you might prefer to paint your model. Many expert builders prefer paint for several reasons. You can match colors precisely. You don't

have any problems with wrinkles, and the finish doesn't sag or bubble. And with the proper technique, you can often make a painted finish come out lighter than an iron-on covering.

There are two types of paints used for models, and they are differentiated by the way they harden. Familiar *enamels* and *dopes* harden by evaporation of the solvent mixed into the paints. *Epoxy paints* harden by chemical action; you mix a hardener with the paint to make this happen.

Recently a series of spray epoxy paints have come onto the market from different manufacturers. These paints require no mixing, but retain some of the harder surface of the mixed epoxy paints. They still dry by evaporation, however.

Paint Brands

Whatever brand of paint you use, you're concerned with *compatibility*. Will it go over the surface you're painting without attacking it? Read the instructions carefully. If you're still not certain, the only sure way to find out is to test it.

When I'm finishing a surface, I like to do a piece of scrap wood the same way as the model. This gives me a piece to test compatibility. I sand it, seal it, and finish it at the same time I do the model. This isn't necessary if you're doing the entire model in an iron-on covering, but if you're using any kind of paint, it can be a lifesaver.

K&B was the first company to make two-part epoxy paints really popular in the hobby industry. They have a wide range of colors. You can change the characteristics of the paint by using different K&B hardeners. There are special hardeners for gloss and matte finishes, and one specifically for brushing. K&B Clear makes an excellent adhesive for fiberglassing.

Perfect Paints are made by Chevron and are sold extensively in hobby shops. They have a very wide range of colors and publish reams of technical reports showing you how to mix their paints to match various military paint schemes.

Hobbypoxy paints are very popular. They're easy to apply and very tough; Hobbypoxy paints were developed for full-size boats, which are harder on their finishes than our planes! Hobbypoxy makes filling putty, Fast Fill grain filler for bare wood, and several grades of epoxy glue. All of these products are compatible with each other, so if you have a

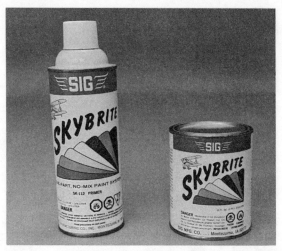

Skybrite is a new paint product from SIG Manufacturing. It's available in cans for brushing or spraying, in a wide range of colors. (Photo courtesy SIG Manufacturing)

problem applying them over each other, it's your own fault.

SIG has produced the most popular brand of dope for many years. Their Supercoat dopes are easily thinned and applied. SIG dopes are available with low-shrink compounds mixed in. They also have nitrate-based dope available, which many people prefer as an undercoat.

SIG offered the Skybrite painting system a few years ago, and it has been very well received. Skybrite paint is available in spray cans or regular cans for brushing. I've had very good success with their spray primer, which covers well and sands very well.

Coverite came out with epoxy paint in spray cans a few years ago. Black Baron Epoxy Paint is now available in cans for brushing as well. One very nice thing about Black Baron paint is that colors are available to match Coverite's iron-on coverings. This is a big help when you're trying to paint a plastic cowl to match the rest of the fuselage!

Thinner

Any paint that doesn't come out of a spray can will go on easier if it's thinned. Thinning helps the pigment spread more easily. Thinned paint is much less likely to be lumpy when it dries. You will also

Hobbypoxy Epoxy Enamel is a two-part paint system; you mix equal parts of Part A and Part B. The resultant paint sets chemically. This gives you a very tough finish. (Photo courtesy *Model Retailer* magazine)

find that two thin coats of paint are lighter than one heavier coat.

If you're using a sprayer or an airbrush, you will probably have to thin 50-50—one part paint to one part thinner. Check the instructions for the paint you're using. You should be aware that overthinned paint can be subject to a problem call *solvent trapping*. This happens when the outer layer of paint dries too fast for the solvent to escape from the paint underneath. Make sure your undercoat and primer are completely dry before you paint, and use thin coats.

Painting Conditions

Any kind of paint will give you trouble if you apply it when the work area is colder than about 70 degrees, or if the humidity is high. Basements are generally poor places to paint for this reason (not to mention the poor ventilation). Paint in your yard on a sunny day. If this is impossible, you can sometimes get away with using a heat lamp to help the paint cure, but be very careful. Too much heat can ruin the finish rapidly.

Surface Preparation

Just as with iron-on coverings, preparing the surface is the most crucial step in painting. Bare wood should be sanded, with all nicks and seams filled in. A filler, such as HobbyPoxy Fast Fill, should be brushed on and sanded two or three times. The key to a good surface isn't how much filler you put on, but how much you sand off. Don't spare the sandpaper!

If you've covered the model with fiberglass cloth, silkspan, Super Coverite, or a similar fabric, be careful not to sand through the fabric. You want to fill in the weave, that's all.

By the way, it's not a good idea to sand over open structure that has been covered, such as wings or stick fuselages. When you sand, the covering will give slightly under the pressure of the sandpaper. The sandpaper will quickly cut through the covering where it touches ribs or stringers. Cover open structures with a covering that doesn't require filling or finishing to accept paint, such as MonoKote or Pre-Primed Micafilm.

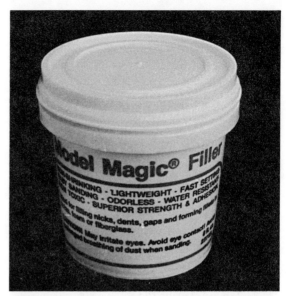

Model Magic Filler comes in small tubs. It's the best thing I've found for covering imperfections and making repairs. It thins with water, dries in half an hour, and sands the same as balsa. (Photo courtesy *Model Retailer* magazine)

Once you've got your filler coats on, vacuum the surface to clear it of dust. Now vacuum your work surface and your clothes, and vacuum the surface again. Get it dust-free . . . it's worth the effort.

Applying Paint

Follow the instructions for the paint you're using to thin it for brushing or spraying, whichever you're planning to do. If you're using a two-part paint, I recommend using a graduated cup for mixing. K&B sells these, and most hobby shops carry them. They make precise measuring a snap. Mix the parts carefully and thoroughly, and let the paint stand for five or ten minutes after mixing to let the chemicals blend thoroughly.

You should use light camel-hair brushes for applying model paints. I like to use wide brushes, since rebrushing most paints doesn't help them. Flow the paint on smoothly. Don't overbrush the areas that you've applied it to; let it smooth out by itself.

Spray painting will almost always give you a better finish than brushing. If you're using a sprayer or airbrush, practice on something to make sure you have enough pressure to do the job right. Shoot on a light mist coat first. Don't stop the spray gun or can before you finish the pass over the surface; overspray both ends. After your light coat is on, go back over it, laying down a heavier coat. It should be wet enough to flow out and cover the surface, but not so heavy as to sag or run.

Holding the spray can or gun at a distance helps you put on much smoother coats. You should be at least two feet away from the surface that's getting the paint.

Trim

The easiest way to put on stripes is with striping tape or trim film. Trim MonoKote is a self-adhesive film that goes over just about everything. Coverite has a whole line of Graphics, trim film that is die-cut in letters, numbers, stripes and stars. I use a lot of Carl Goldberg Color Stripe, a very thin tape that is flexible enough to make good corners. All of these products have a type of adhesive that doesn't develop its maximum strength for a few hours, so unless the surface you're applying it to is fragile, you can lift and reposition them.

When you apply striping tape, be very careful not to stretch it. If you pull it tight, it'll inevitably shrink back and pull away at the ends. Work the tape around a curve gradually, pulling it up and pushing it down again until the outer edge of the tape stretches smoothly around the corner.

Masking

If you want to paint your detail color, there are a few tips you should use when you're masking the area to be painted. Ordinary masking tape will grab pretty tightly. Be very careful when you pull the tape up; pull it back on itself at a very sharp angle, and work slowly. If you're concerned about pulling up your base color, you can use drafting tape instead of masking tape; this is made of the same kind of paper as masking tape, but has a much lighter grab.

To avoid having paint creep under the edge of the tape, I like to rub it down lightly with a blunt piece of wood. A very light coat of clear spray, such as Black Baron Clear, will seal the edges very effectively. Be certain that whatever spray you use is compatible with the undercoat.

If I'm using dope, I leave the masking tape in place until the dope is dry. With other paints, I take the tape up soon as I'm finished applying it. This allows the edge of the paint that's left to flatten itself out, and gives me a chance to remove any spots where the paint has crept under the tape.

If you want a really sharp edge between color areas, use striping tape that matches one color or the other. This is a handy trick for covering a seam between two iron-on films, too.

FIBERGLASS CLOTH

If you are building a plane with very little open framework in the structure, you might want to consider fiberglassing it. Applying a coat of fiberglass will greatly strengthen the surface of the wood, and make it much more resistant to dings and scratches. This is also very useful over foam wings. Most paints go over a fiberglassed surface very easily, and getting the surface smooth enough to paint is much easier than filling the wood grain or the surface of the foam with a brush-on filler. You can lay on the fiberglass cloth in a couple of simple steps, and it takes only the lightest sanding to prepare it for the final coat.

Grades of Fiberglass Cloth

You can buy fiberglass cloth in several different grades, differentiated by the weight of the cloth. K&B makes three grades: light, medium and, heavy. Other sources offer even lighter weights. Look for small ads in the model magazines that offer ultra-light cloth. It's expensive, so I use it most where there are tight corners or curves. I've bought ultra-light glass cloth from Dan Parsons, 11809 Fulmer Dr. NE, Albuquerque, NM 87111.

I use the lightest grade I can get for most applications. The lighter the cloth, the more easily it drapes around curves and tucks into corners. And of course it will add less weight to the structure.

Heavy cloth is used for reinforcing areas that need strength. A two-inch wide strip of heavy glass cloth glued around the joint between two wing panels will greatly strengthen the wing and add relatively little weight.

Fiberglass cloth is adhered to the surface with thinned epoxy or epoxy paint. Work from the center of the surface to the edges, being careful not to trap air underneath. (Photo by Jennifer Pratt)

Medium cloth can be used to toughen surfaces that might be abused in use. A layer of this cloth along the bottom of a fuselage will add a lot of scuff resistance in the event of a bad landing.

Applying Fiberglass

Before you apply fiberglass cloth, make sure you've sanded the surface until it's smooth. Glassing won't cover glue ridges, bumps, or seams. Use a light grade of sandpaper for final smoothing, and vacuum the surface to remove the dust.

There are several epoxies on the market that work well for fiberglassing. I've used K&B Clear Epoxy paint with excellent success. Some people like to use an ordinary 30-minute epoxy, thinned to brushing consistency with alcohol.

PIC Coating Poxy is a new product on the market just for fiberglassing. It mixes to a good brush-ing consistency right out of the bottle. It's also free of the wax that ordinary epoxy glues sometimes have that make them difficult to sand.

Many modelers use polyester resin for fiber-glassing. I don't care for it, because of the MEK catalyst it uses. MEK Peroxide can blind you very quickly if any gets in your eyes. If you use polyester resin, be sure to wear eye protection.

Cut a piece of glass cloth larger by ¼ inch all the way around than the surface you are covering. Starting at one corner, brush the epoxy through the cloth and onto the surface. Work slowly until you have the corner secured. Now work across the sur-face, being careful not to trap air bubbles under the cloth.

To work around corners and curves, go slowly and use the brush to make sure the glass is right down on the surface. If you can, start with the

Light fiberglass cloth will drape right around corners easily. When you have the entire surface adhered, work around the corners, brushing out any wrinkles. (Photo by Jennifer Pratt)

When your fiberglass is attached, and a filler coat has been brushed on and sanded off, you're ready to spray paint. (Photo by Jennifer Pratt)

corners so that there's no tension on the cloth as you're adhering it at the most difficult point. When you finish the panel, look at the corners again to be certain that you haven't inadvertently pulled the cloth up from the corner. This is easy to correct while the epoxy is still soft.

Sanding and Finishing Glass Cloth

Once the cloth is on and the epoxy has set, it will usually require a coat of clear epoxy paint or something similar to totally fill the weave. You should sand very lightly before applying this coat; sand just enough to remove any bumps or ridges, being sure not to sand down into the cloth. Seams and over-laps should be sanded out now; they will feather out flat very quickly.

I like to use a primer at this point, such as Hob-byPoxy Fast Fill or SIG Skybrite Primer. Both sand very well. Since the Skybrite is a spray, it will prob-ably require two coats.

Once your primer is down and sanded, inspect the surface under a bright light. Sand out any rough spots now. When you're happy, apply color coats.

Chapter 6

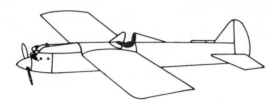

Flying: The Proof of the Pudding

IT WAS A PERFECT DAY, AND I WAS READY TO FLY. But something wasn't quite right. I hunted around for the fault and found something that worried me; one aileron had hinges that were starting to come loose. It might not have caused a problem in the air, and I sure hated to waste that beautiful day, but I chickened out and started packing up the plane. An old flying buddy of mine consoled me with this rule: "It's a lot better to be down here wishing you were up there, than up there wishing you were down here."

ARE YOU READY?

If your plane has been built straight, and the engine and radio installed properly, and the whole works has been checked over by an expert friend, then *yes,* you're ready. At least, your airplane is. You'll probably need some emotional preflight checkout, too.

The help of an expert friend is very important. Someone else will almost always spot something that your eye passes over; proofreaders learn this early. I always ask someone else to look over my plane the first time I bring it out. Don't be afraid to ask for this courtesy from your fellow fliers; most of the "experts" do it, too.

YOUR PREFLIGHT CHECKLIST

Here is a list of things that you should do before you fly. It's based on a lot of experience—my own and that of many others.

Before Mounting the Wing

Inspect each servo linkage. Tighten the screw that holds the servo output arm. If you've used pushrod connectors that have a screw that tightens down on the pushrod, check these for tightness.

Look at the battery pack and receiver. Have they come out of their protective foam wrapping?

Check each servo lead where it plugs into the receiver. Is it still plugged all the way in?

Club flying fields are great places to meet your friends and see what they're flying. You'll learn a lot, and enjoy yourself too.

Inspect for cracks in the fuselage or any signs of fuel or oil leaks. Oil will work its way under the wing or through openings in the engine compartment, and will eventually weaken the wood.

Check your wing attachment system. If you use nylon bolts, are the mounting blocks securely glued to the fuselage? If you use rubber bands, are the retaining dowels cracked or bent?

After Mounting the Wing

Is part of the aileron servo wire peeking out from under one wing? Is the wing seated firmly in place?

Look at all the clevises and control horns. Clevises can come unsnapped, which puts a lot of strain on the clevis pin. Horns can come loose, too. Each of your clevises should be "safetied" with a bit of fuel tubing, as described in Chapter 4.

Grab the vertical fin and wiggle it. Do the same to the stabilizer. Are they still firmly glued? Sometimes the tail of a plane takes a real beating in the trunk of your car on the way to the field!

Tug gently on each aileron, on the elevator, and on the rudder. Look at the hinges as you do this. Are any of them starting to pull loose? The force of the air can pull a control surface right off the plane if the hinges aren't firmly glued in and pinned.

Check each wheel. Does it rotate smoothly? Is the wheel collar set screw tight? I've had wheels fall off in flight; it's embarrassing, and it makes landings more interesting than they ought to be.

Did your landing gear get bent the last time you landed? It can make the plane handle poorly during taxi and takeoff.

Walk a few paces to the front of the plane and look straight at it. Check for a crookedly mounted wing or other obvious problems. Do the same to the rear of the plane.

The Engine

Give the engine compartment the once-over. Is the throttle connection tight? Losing throttle control may not crash your plane, but it won't make the flight more fun, either.

Check the engine mounting bolts. These take more vibration than most other components and can loosen quickly when the engine is running.

Check the muffler bolts. I've seen a lot of mufflers bail out in mid-flight!

Check the prop and spinner. Examine the prop for cracks. *Never* use a cracked prop!

Pick up the plane and shake it gently side-to-side. You should be able to hear the klunk weight at the end of the fuel pickup in the tank as it moves from side to side. Klunks sometimes get wedged against one corner of the tank.

Disconnect the tank pressure line from the muffler, and fuel line from the carburetor. If you're not using muffler pressure, check to be sure the vent line won't spray fuel where it isn't wanted as the tank fills.

Fill the tank. As you do, watch for leaks and cracks in the fuel line.

Hook up the pressure line to the muffler (if used) and the fuel line to the carburetor. Make sure these lines are as straight as possible, and that there are no kinks to restrict fuel flow.

Control Checkout

Put the plane on the ground. Get your frequency pin and switch on your transmitter. Now switch on your receiver and move all the controls. Watch for

The Super Cradle comes in handy on the field, as a convenient place to assemble and check out your plane. (Photo by Jennifer Pratt)

84

smoothness of operation; jerky movement can indicate a loose pushrod or a servo with problems.

Check to make sure your controls all move in the proper directions! Even the experts sometimes take off with the ailerons working backwards. This is especially important if your radio has switches that reverse the servo's direction of rotation. Those switches can get moved, and the best time to discover it is *now*.

Range Checking the Radio

You can't put your transmitter on a spectrum analyzer and your receiver on an oscilloscope before every flying session, but you can perform a very simple test that will help spot abnormal conditions before you discover them in the air.

With your plane on the ground and the radio system on, fully collapse your transmitter antenna. This reduces the power output to a very low level. Stand at the front of the plane, looking down at it. Now walk away from the plane, counting your paces. Every few steps, turn and face the plane, pointing the collapsed antenna directly at it. Since most of the radio energy radiates from the sides of the antenna, this makes it even harder for the receiver to hear the transmitter. Move the controls. Sooner or later, you'll be too far away from the plane to control it properly. The surfaces will move jerkily, or not at all.

Now walk slowly back toward the plane until you regain solid control. Remember the number of paces it takes to get to this point. You should be 40 or 50 feet away from the the the plane right now. If you're of average height, you probably stride 2 ½ feet, so you should be 15 to 20 paces from the plane.

You're standing on the ground, with your antenna collapsed, and the plane is on the ground, too. You're pointing the antenna at the plane. This is the worst position for the radio link. If you have good range under these conditions, you'll be in good shape in the air.

Range check your plane every time you bring it out to the field. If you find that range is less than it was the last time you checked, look for other problems. There will be variations due to terrain, high humidity, and other factors that affect radio waves, but these should be barely noticeable.

Range checking your radio should be done every time you go flying. With the transmitter antenna collapsed, see how far away you can get and still control the plane. If you notice a drop in range, check out the radio system carefully. (Photo by Jennifer Pratt)

Pete Waters, owner and operator of Kraft Midwest, a major radio system repair business, pointed out to me that range checks are most valuable if they're always done in the same place. If you always range check at the same spot, your system will always "see" the same terrain and surroundings. It'll be easier to remember exactly how far away you got before the servos started to jitter. If you range test a system at the field, then take it home to your back yard and do the same check, you will probably see a quite different range. This can get really confusing! So try to range check your system in the same spot each time.

Checking the Batteries

I assume that you charged your batteries the night before your flying session. Check Chapter 3 for information on the care and feeding of your system batteries, and the equipment and procedures you need to check them out in the shop. But you also need to be able to check battery condition on the field, before you fly.

As we discussed in Chapter 3, ni-cad batteries don't discharge at an even rate. They maintain a relatively high voltage until they're just about out of juice, then the voltage drops quickly. They also bounce up to a higher voltage if they aren't under load; in other words, if they aren't actually putting power into something, they'll show a higher voltage than they can actually deliver when called upon to work. So you need to be able to check the transmitter and receiver batteries under load, with a device sensitive enough to spot minor changes in voltage.

The transmitter is no problem. When you switch it on, check the meter. It'll show you the state of the batteries, usually with a green-yellow-and-red range to indicate when it's safe to fly. The transmitter batteries never have to cope with varying power loads, since the transmitter circuitry draws the same power no matter where the sticks or other controls are set. So transmitter batteries seldom cause trouble, except at the end of a long day's flying—or if they were accidentally left off the charger the night before.

The receiver battery is a different story. It has to do more than supply steady power to the receiver. Each servo contains an electric motor that draws all its power from the receiver pack. If one of these motors encounters resistance, it draws more power. If for some reason it stalls, or comes up against something it can't move, it draws a whole lot of power and can drain your receiver battery in a matter of minutes.

So the rate at which you discharge your receiver battery will depend on two main factors: how long the receiver is switched on and how much work the servos do. If you're flying a sailplane that doesn't fly fast (so the servos don't have to push as hard), your receiver battery will last longer. On a fast aerobatic machine flown through plenty of high-speed maneuvers, the pack can be drained in a few flights.

You can solve a lot of potential battery drain

problems as you build. See Chapter 4 for more information on how to avoid stalling servos by properly laying out your pushrods and control runs.

I like to check my receiver battery pack before every third flight. I make it a definite rule not to fly more than four flights without checking or charging the receiver pack.

There are several very handy devices on the market to help you check your receiver pack. They are often called ESVs, or expanded scale voltmeters. *Expanded scale* means that the voltmeter is designed to show a very small change of voltage. Some ESVs use meters; others use some form of digital readout. All of them put a load on the battery pack to check the voltage while the battery is working. You connect an ESV to your receiver pack through the charging jack. You're looking for two things: the voltage level, and how quickly it drops. If the voltage reads in the green area of the meter, okay so far. Leave the ESV connected for about 60 seconds. If the voltage drops more than about .2 volt, you should think twice before flying.

Don't leave an ESV plugged in for more than a couple of minutes. The resistor in the ESV will get warm, and you'll drain the receiver pack.

THE PIT AREA

The club flying field will have a designated pit area where you can lay out your airplane, fuel, equipment, lawn chair, and cooler. This is an area that is supposedly free of spectators (who have a tendency to trip over things) where you can assemble your plane and check it over.

Many fields don't permit you to start or run your engine in the pits, but have a designated area off to the side for this. This is to avoid problems if your engine backfires and the prop nut and spinner come flying off, or if your prop should happen to shed a blade. You should respect these rules and avoid the temptation to run your engine right next to all your equipment in the pits. At the club field where I fly, starting the engine in the pit is permissible. Once you have it going, you taxi or carry the plane to a spot halfway between the pit and the flight line for engine runup.

RUNNING UP THE ENGINE

Model engines ought to be run up to full throttle for a moment and checked before each flight, even if you just came down a few minutes ago for more fuel. Why? For the same reason that you wiggle your controls before each takeoff. It's your last chance to spot a brewing problem before it turns into an in-flight emergency.

Model engines like to warm up, and the time spent idling and testing before takeoff is helpful. Here are some simple checks you can perform quickly to help the engine settle into the groove.

First, straddle the airplane behind the wing, with the stabilizer touching your ankles. This may appear awkward, but it's very unlikely that the plane will get away from you when you're holding it like this. Now slowly advance the throttle, watching the engine all the while. Does it move from idle to high speed smoothly, or does it sag out as you start to advance the throttle? Sagging is a sign that the needle valve is set too rich and needs to be turned in a couple of clicks. When it's at high speed, does it roar smoothly, or does it start to sag after 10 seconds of full speed? Sagging at full throttle probably indicates that the engine is too lean and the needle valve needs to be backed out a couple of clicks. You can lean forward, holding the transmitter in one hand, and perform the necessary adjustments on the needle valve with very little risk of sticking your finger in the prop. Remember, *all* adjustments to the needle valve *must* be done from behind the engine. *Never* reach around a spinning prop to tweak a needle valve...sooner or later you could slash your wrists that way. When dealing with moving propellers, you can never be too careful.

This is a good time to spot engine mount bolts and muffler attachment bolts that are getting ready to let go. If you see bolt heads jiggling, stop everything and tighten them up. If your muffler leaves the party from 50 feet in the air, it's going to be very hard to locate . . . especially since you can't take your eyes off the plane to see where the muffler went!

Okay, the engine is holding its speed and sounding good at full throttle. Set the transmitter on the ground. Grasp the plane firmly by the leading edge of the wing (watch out for oil from the exhaust, which can make your hand slip) and point the nose of the plane up in the air. It doesn't have to be straight up, but point it as high up as you can get it without getting too close to the prop. Hold the plane in this position for 10 seconds or so. Does the engine sag out and sound like it's going to quit? It's too lean. Does the engine speed up and run happily at a slightly higher speed? The needle valve is set slightly on the rich side, which is right where you want it.

Put the plane back on the ground and pick up the transmitter. Quickly reduce the throttle to idle. Does the engine sound as if it's going to quit? If it's too lean, it'll sometimes quit entirely when you do this. You might have to adjust the idle mixture, a procedure that varies with the type of engine you have; see the chapters on engines for details of this.

The purpose of these exercises is to detect a too-lean engine before takeoff. All engines run leaner once they're in the air, because the prop unloads. They lean out when the nose of the plane points up, because fuel flow is slightly reduced by gravity. When you take off, you get both of these conditions at once; the prop starts pulling the plane, and the nose goes up. Having your engine quit just as you start to gain some altitude means an unplanned landing. It happens to all of us; I had it happen to me just a few weeks ago, with a plane that I had flown twice that day, because I neglected to follow my own preflight procedures. (We'll discuss what to do when an engine fails on takeoff in just a minute, under Takeoffs.)

TAXIING

Point your plane in the direction you want to go, and carefully add throttle. Practice turning the plane until you have a good feel for how tight a turn you can make. In fact, if you have the chance, you should practice taxiing up and down the runway a few times. If your field is too busy for this, do it in another suitable area.

If your plane has a nosewheel, you'll discover how tightly you can turn without tilting the plane up on its nose. When you built the plane you might have been concerned about how little the nosewheel seemed to turn. Once you start taxiing around, you realize that it doesn't take much movement of the

CORRECT

CORRECT

INCORRECT

When you start your engine, have a helper holding the model firmly. Adjust the engine from the rear. Never reach around the engine from the front. Watch out for loose clothing that can get caught in the prop! (Illustration by Hank Clark, used by permission of Altech Marketing) nosewheel to make the plane taxi where you want it to.

If your plane is a taildragger, you'll discover that holding about half up elevator helps keep the tail on the ground and greatly improves steerability. It also slows the plane down quite a lot. If you suddenly let the elevator return to neutral, you'll be surprised how quickly the plane will move forward. And it may very well nose over and stop the engine. Practice until you can make it go where you want with no danger of nosing over.

I've built a lot of taildragger airplanes, and I've always found that they are perfectly easy to maneuver on the ground. This is true whether they have a fixed tailskid or one that is attached to the rudder and moves with it. Whether you have a fixed or steerable tailskid (or tailwheel), check it frequently to make sure that it tracks straight with the rest of the plane. Skids can get bent off to one side or the other, making the plane pull to one side during the takeoff run.

Taxiing a new plane around is a lot of fun, since there's very little chance of doing it any damage. It's useful, too, so you have some good excuses to go out and play with the plane without actually flying it. As you putt around on the grass, observe the way the controls work. If the plane consistently pulls to one side or the other, check to be sure that the wheels spin freely on the axles. If the plane is a taildragger, the wheel axles should be in line with or slightly ahead of the leading edge of the wing. If they are very far behind the leading edge, the plane will tend to nose over a lot and be very tricky to land. You can experiment with giving the engine quick bursts with the rudder hard over to blow the tail around to the left or right. That's a technique that full-scale taildragger pilots use; of course, it's easier for them since they can use wheel brakes! (So can you if you want to install them; DuBro makes the parts to add brakes to your plane.)

Once you're comfortable with the plane's ground handling, make some simulated takeoff runs. Line it up straight at one end of the runway, and slowly add throttle. When the plane starts to roll, concentrate on keeping it tracking in a straight line. Shut down the throttle when you get halfway up the runway, or if the plane shows any tendency to get light on its feet. Make a few runs in this manner, with a little more throttle each time. Practice until you're sure you can add the rudder necessary to track straight down the runway every time. This will also teach you at what speed the plane will become airborne, and whether or not you'll have to use a touch of up elevator to unstick the wheels from the ground.

Now you can get a bit braver, if you have a long enough runway, and practice becoming airborne for brief hops. As you do this, watch for any tendency for the plane to roll either left or right. A roll like this could indicate a warped wing. As the plane breaks ground, you'll have to learn to release the rudder you were holding to keep it tracking straight on the ground. Learn this with brief hops and let your confidence build.

Taildraggers are trickier to handle here, as you'll discover, but you can learn more from taxiing them. You have to discover how much up elevator the plane needs to keep the tail from coming up too fast as it builds up speed and nosing over onto the prop. If you hold too much up, the plane will take off from a three-point stance, which can be right on the edge of a stall. Learn to make high-speed taxis with your taildragger up on its main wheels, tracking straight down the runway, settling back down when you chop the throttle. Once you have this down pat, taking off will be a piece of cake.

TAKEOFF

You'll sometimes see fliers walk out onto the runway and stand behind their plane as they take off. They get into the habit, and some claim this makes it easier for them to correct any rolling to the right or left as the plane breaks ground. I don't like this practice for several reasons. For one thing, once the plane takes off, you either have to have a friend beside you to lead you back to the pilot area at the side of the runway, or you have to try to walk back there and watch the plane at the same time. It also makes it harder to judge how steeply the plane is pointing its nose in the air. I really feel that it's better practice to stand in the pilot area, get yourself positioned and comfortable while your plane is idling on the taxiway, and then taxi out to the end of the runway for takeoff.

Common courtesy (and sometimes club rules) dictates that you should make your intentions known to the other pilots on the flight line. They're concentrating on their airplanes, and can't take a minute to glance over and see if you're on the runway. Announce your intentions by saying "I'm on the field" or something like that in a loud voice.

The pilots who are already in the air have the right of way. If one of them is preparing to land, or has his engine quit ("dead stick"), you must wait for him to make his landing before you may taxi out onto the active runway. You will get the same courtesy from him later.

You'll find that most RC flight lines have marked spots for the pilot to stand on while flying. AMA's Frequency Committee recommends that these spots be at least 20 feet apart. This is because the signals from two transmitters on different channels can combine to cause interference on a third channel, a phenomenon known as *third-order intermodulation.* If you want to know more about this, see Chapter 2 of *The Advanced Guide to Radio Control Sport Flying* (TAB Book #3060), or Appendix F. But even if you don't understand what makes it happen, it's important that you know that it's there. Furthermore, third-order intermodulation disappears when the two transmitters that are producing it are moved apart. At 20 feet of separation between transmitters, it should be negligible. So don't stand right next to the other guys on the flight line!

After you've practiced hopping the plane, takeoff is the natural next step. Position yourself at the end of the runway, facing into whatever wind is blowing. Advance the throttle slowly, as you practiced. Keep the plane tracking straight; if it veers to one side or the other, chop the throttle and start over at the end of the runway. Your practice sessions will help keep you from over controlling.

You're headed down the runway at about half throttle, looking good. Smoothly add throttle until the wheels leave the ground. Release any rudder you were using to keep the plane tracking straight, and hold enough elevator to ascend smoothly in a shallow climb. Once you're high enough to be com-

fortable with it, make a left turn (away from the flight line) and move out into the flight area, where you can enjoy yourself.

If you checked your engine as we described earlier, it should not have sagged out or quit when you took off. An engine failure on takeoff can be merely an embarrassment, if you're lucky enough to have a field with a clear space beyond the runway to put the plane down. Don't panic. Don't try to pull the nose up or stretch the glide. Airspeed is your most important consideration at this point, and in order to maintain airspeed, you need to keep the nose low. Don't try to turn! Turning takes a lot of airspeed, and you can easily stall the plane right into the ground at this point. Pretend that there's a runway underneath the plane, and land on it.

BASIC MANEUVERS

There are a few basic maneuvers you need to master in order to make the plane do what you want it to. More importantly, they help you discover what the plane is capable of, and can show you potential problems. As we go through these basics, I'll describe things to watch for that will tell you to make certain changes or adjustments to the plane. Being able to analyze a plane in flight like this will serve you well in the future!

What the Controls Do

When you first look at an RC plane, it looks simple: the rudder turns it right and left, the ailerons are for making it fly level, the throttle makes it go faster or slower, and the elevator makes it go up and down. *Wrong on all counts.* Working together, all of these controls make it do all of these things, but it isn't as simple as that.

The relationship between throttle and elevator is important. It's exactly the reverse of what a beginner expects: Throttle controls *altitude,* and elevator controls *airspeed.* The combination of the two determines how high, how fast, and in what attitude the plane will fly. This interaction is easy to understand when you understand another basic rule; altitude and airspeed are interchangeable. To get one, you give up some of the other.

Turns

When you consider it, you'll see that a model plane spends most of its time in turning flight, rather than straight wings-level attitude, so the way a plane handles itself in a turn is most important.

You can get in trouble in a turn in a number of ways. If you turn too tightly, some planes will stall the lower wing, resulting in a sudden snap roll. A less extreme effect (thought still disconcerting) of this is the tendency to increase the angle of bank, often called "dropping the wingtip." You will find yourself fighting to make the bank more shallow by applying opposite aileron, while adding more up elevator to keep the nose from dropping too. This can stall both wings!

In any case, you need to be aware of good turning technique. You should practice making turns until you can put the plane in any turning attitude and you know what to expect.

Follow me through a typical right turn in a trainer plane equipped with ailerons. First we feed in right aileron to bank the plane. We add aileron until the plane is about at a 45-degree angle. Then, still holding right stick, we pull the stick back gently. This gives us up elevator and actually starts the plane turning. If we want a tighter turn, we add more up elevator; a shallower turn, we let the stick move back toward the center a little. Meanwhile, we are holding as much right aileron as the plane needs to maintain its angle of bank. At this point, halfway through the turn, it probably needs less right aileron than we started with.

Now the nose is swinging around to the heading we want the plane to be on at the end of the turn. Still holding up elevator, we move the stick through neutral to left aileron. The plane levels its wings. As this happens, less up elevator is required. We let the stick move forward, and when the wings are level we let the ailerons return to neutral. We have held enough up elevator to keep the nose level in the last part of the turn, since here is where it will show a tendency to drop.

If you run through this maneuver in your mind, you'll see that we moved the stick in a sort of down-facing D. We started moving it to the right, swung it down and to the center as the plane proceeded through the turn, and ended up opposite where we started, on the left; then let it return to neutral.

As you practice this maneuver, you'll learn how much elevator and aileron to hold through this procedure for your particular plane. All planes are different in the precise ways they react to control inputs. You'll probably horse the plane around a bit while you're feeling it out, but you'll have it smoothed out quickly; it's a very natural action.

Turning Three-Channel Planes

Three-channel airplanes (rudder, elevator and throttle controls only) don't have ailerons. They turn by using the rudder to rock the wings to the left or right. You'll find that they will respond in a very similar manner to the aileron plane described above. The only noticeable difference is that not as much up elevator is required, and adding elevator won't tighten the turn significantly. Concentrate on using the elevator to keep the nose level. The nose will show a strong tendency to drop in the middle of a turn on this kind of airplane.

APPROACH AND LANDING

It's time to think about landing. The best way to land a plane is to allow it to sink onto the runway with its nose still level. Different planes will sink at different rates. You can experiment with your plane to discover the right combination of throttle and elevator to make it sink. Set up an approach, except rather than being at the right altitude, start out considerably higher than you would if you really intended to hit the runway. Holding the nose level with up elevator, reduce throttle to idle. As the plane slows, continue to hold the nose up with more elevator. Soon you'll see it start to settle toward the ground, perfectly level. Be careful not to point the nose up, or you'll risk slowing the plane past its stalling speed and inviting a snap roll. Stand by the throttle control, and add power again once you've seen where the sink begins and how fast the plane comes down. Do this a few times out in front of you, where you can watch the plane and are comfortable controlling it.

Now practice making runs at the runway. Fly

the square pattern; parallel the runway, then turn onto your downwind leg. Make your turn onto final at half throttle. Reduce throttle to idle when you're lined up with the runway. Hold the nose up just as you did when you were experimenting with making the plane sink. If you get it right, it'll sink right onto the runway for a "three point" landing. If not, be ready to slowly add throttle and do a missed approach or "go-around."

All the while you're doing this, keep your wings level with the ailerons. This can often be the trickiest part of making your approach, and that's why you should practice making approaches until you can keep the plane on the proper heading straight down the runway. I had difficulties with this on my first powered plane. A friend suggested that I tell myself to "point the stick at the low wing" while I'm on approach. In other words, if I'm coming in and the right wing starts to drop, I move the aileron stick to the right to level the wings. It worked, and the plane survived long enough for me to develop the reflexes to keep the wings level whether it was coming at me or going away.

Practice, practice, practice. Make your first approaches high so you have plenty of room to recover as you feel out the plane. Remember what the professional pilots say: "Nothing is more useless than altitude above you, unless it's fuel left on the ground." You will soon learn how your plane likes you to control it in all speed ranges.

Once your wheels touch the ground, your plane becomes a land vehicle and you have to shift mental gears to accommodate it. Forget the aileron and start using the rudder to steer. Plaster the wheels on the ground by letting the elevator come back down. Hold just enough up elevator to keep the plane from nosing over; you don't want too much, or you may find that you have enough speed to go right back up in the air.

Now you're taxiing, just as you practiced before your first takeoff. You should be good at this by now.

GROUND EQUIPMENT

There are lots of different items that you can carry with you to the field for ground support. I'll discuss the essential ones first, then look at some of the conveniences.

Field Boxes

The first thing you'll need is something to carry your junk to the field with. A shoebox will do the trick at first, but it won't be long before you want something better.

There are several field boxes of varying sizes on the market. The smallest one is the Handi-Tote from Carl Goldberg Models. It has a drawer, a box on top with holes for tools, a transmitter carrier, a spot for a tank of fuel, and another spot for a battery. There are two wire racks that support a small plane on the top; these are removable. I have two of these, one for electric flying and the other for diesel engine supplies.

Most fliers need a little more than this. Your dealer will show you quite a range of boxes, with a lot of different features. I've gotten a lot of good use out of a box made by AeroTrend. It's made of fiberglass, with a hinged lid that drops down to form a tray. Three drawers hold small parts. Two very solid clamps hold the plane at a good spot for me to work on it without bending over. It even has folding legs on the bottom. This box stands in the corner of my workshop when it's not on the field.

Another very useful box I have is from Ultra Systems. Ultra makes a wide range of boxes notable for their excellent plane supports. They can hold a plane of any size or shape at any angle. I use one of these near my workbench to hold the fuselage while I install the radio or work on the engine. Many Ultra boxes have a built-in paper towel rack, a real help at the end of the day.

Generally speaking, you should look for a field box that has a couple of drawers to hold bits and pieces. It should have a good place to put your starter and the 12-volt battery necessary to run it. If you plan to use a power panel (see below), pick a box with a spot to install the panel and a secure, vented compartment for the 12-volt battery. Legs are nice, since you'll get really tired of bending over all day long. The best stands support your model at the right height to work on it at the field. The supports must be secure. If they're at all weak or

A field box is handy for carrying equipment and spare parts out to the field. Most boxes have room for a battery, starter, fuel pump, and small parts. Some support the airplane for testing and engine running. (Photo by Jennifer Pratt)

wobbly, don't start the engine before you remove the plane and set it on the ground.

Glow Plug Battery

You will need to connect a 1½-volt battery to your glow plug to start the engine. There are several different devices that do this. You can use a dry battery, but this will run down before long. Most of the people I fly with use small recharegable batteries that have a glow plug connector attached directly to them. The most popular of these is the Ni-Starter, manufactured by McDaniel RC and sold in hobby stores. It charges overnight, and is good for several days of average use between charges. Another popular product of this type is the Nilite 2, made by Ace RC. They both attach to the plug with a fitting called a Head Lock, which locks in place by twisting

slightly. If you find another brand of glow plug battery, look closely at the mechanism that locks it onto the plug. That's the most important part. Some simply jam on, and can pop off once the engine starts shaking.

It's often useful to have a meter on the plug battery. A voltmeter will show you that the battery isn't flat and is delivering the voltage to the plug. McDaniel makes a Metered Ni-Starter that has a voltmeter, the battery, and the Head Lock in a neat stack. Ace RC's Nilite 3 is similar.

Many fliers go a step beyond a simple battery and use a device called a *glow driver*. These circuits are capable of varying the current delivered to the plug; some do this automatically, others are adjustable with a knob. Most of such circuits are enclosed in a power panel, a device that fits into your range box and is powered by a 12-volt battery.

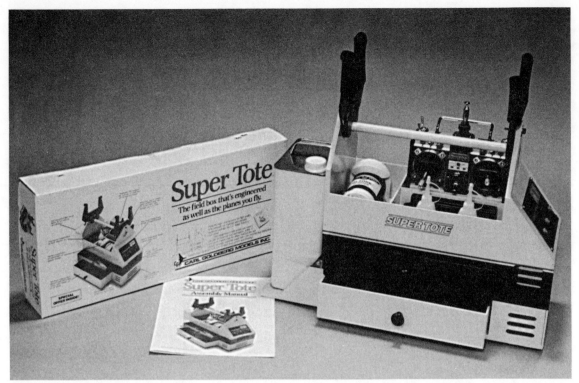

Carl Goldberg Models makes three field boxes of different sizes. The newest one is the Super Tote, which can carry a 12-volt battery, power panel, fuel can, pump, parts and tools. (Photo courtesy *Model Retailer* magazine)

Fuel Pump

You're going to need some method of getting fuel into the tank. The simplest and cheapest method is a fuel bulb. These are made of rubber, and have brass spouts to connect your fuel line to. They seldom break, and they work whether your battery is charged or not. I carry one in my range box as a spare. It also comes in very handy for squirting a few drops of fuel into a carb to prime it, or blowing air into the engine exhaust port to help clear a flood.

The next simplest type of fuel pump is the hand crank type. I've used two different ones, one made by Dave Brown Products and the other made by Du-Bro. They both work very well. They attach to the side of a fuel jug or can with a strap, and the tubes fit into holes in the can cap. You just unplug one line from the cap, attach it to your plane's tank, and start cranking. The Dave Brown "Six Shooter" pump is available in a model that will pump gasoline and diesel fuel as well as glow fuel.

Finally, for those of us who are as lazy as we can manage, there are electric fuel pumps. These usually require either 6 or 12-volt batteries as power sources. Most power panels have the appropriate connections to power and control a pump. This is really the ultimate in convenience.

There are a lot of electric fuel pumps available. I've used several and had good results with all. My favorite is a Mark X, made by Sonic-Tronics. This pump is sold in 6 or 12-volt models, with or without a switch mounted on the pump itself. If you have a power panel, you don't need the switch.

I have a 6-volt Mark X pump. I glued it to the case of a large five-cell ni-cad pack, and made it completely portable. It's worked for over four years with no sign of leaking.

Clean-Up

Finally, you'll need supplies to clean the exhaust oil off your plane when the day's flying is over. I carry a roll of paper towels, plus some rags to wrap around each engine so no oil drips onto my van carpet.

A spray cleaner is a must. You want a cleaner that cuts through oil, since most of the exhaust is castor oil or other lubricant. Avoid any cleaner with abrasives. I favor Windex and Formula 409. Small bottles fit in the range box better, and can always be refilled from the household supply when your wife isn't looking.

Starters and Chicken Sticks

It may seem like a lot of money to spend at first, but I recommend that you buy a starter. A good one will last you for years, and pay for itself several times over in good service. In my experience, Sullivan makes the best starters.

You also need to buy a chicken stick for flipping the prop. I know you'll see people on the field flipping props by hand. You're also likely to see those same folks with bandages on their flipping fingers sooner or later. If you flip a prop with your finger you are sure to get whacked sooner or later. Why ask for it? Use a chicken stick, and only turn the prop over by hand when you're firmly holding the prop between your thumb and forefinger.

12-Volt Batteries

Modelers use 12-volt batteries for three main purposes: to power the starter, to run the fuel pump, and to light the glow plug. They can also come in handy for running various field charging devices.

If you don't want to bother with a 12-volt battery, you can easily get along without one. Using a rechargeable glow plug battery such as the NiStarter will mean you don't need a power panel. And there are several different kits around to power your starter with a pack of 10 sub-C size ni-cad cells. There's even a device called a Bump Starter that starts engines without any battery at all. It contains a powerful spring. You wind it up by cranking the starter cone backwards, and when you push it against the engine spinner, the spring is released and it turns over the motor.

If you want a 12-volt battery you have two choices: a small lead-acid battery or a sealed cell "gellcell" type. The small lead-acid batteries are generally the same size used in small motorcycles. They have to be filled with electrolyte and maintained just like a car battery. The "gellcell" batteries use a gelled electrolyte and are completely sealed. They require no maintenance other than charging.

Of the two, I highly recommend the gellcell. It can't be spilled, it won't produce acid unless you break it, and its generally a bit smaller and lighter than the same size wet cell battery.

Charging these batteries is different from charging ni-cad cells. Unlike a ni-cad, which can sit in a partially-charged state for months, a lead-acid battery will die for good unless it's kept at a good state of charge. You have to be aware of this and deal with it.

The charger you usually get with a 12-volt battery is intended to bring it up to full charge overnight. You should put the battery on it for a few hours every month if you're not using the battery regularly to make sure the battery hasn't gotten discharged.

I strongly recommend getting a charger that will go automatically to a trickle charge rate when it senses that the battery is well charged. The Ace RC "CVC" (Constant Voltage Charger) is the one I use. I built it from a kit and saved a few bucks. It senses the state of charge of the battery and delivers charge current accordingly. You can leave your battery on the CVC for weeks at a time—and I do.

Tachometers

A tachometer will help you get the best performance from your engine. They're well-nigh essential for setting four-stroke engines to a proper needle valve setting. But you can get along without one for years, too. It's up to you; if you're a beginner, ask for one for Christmas.

There are lots of tachometers on the market. I favor the ones that use a photocell to count the number of times a prop blade goes by, rather than ones that have you push a cone against the spinner. They're much safer and easier to use, and they work very well from behind the prop, which is the best place to be when tuning the engine.

I've used several tachs with good success. The Nor Cal Accu-Tach is a very compact unit that doubles as a digital voltmeter, and has circuitry to apply a load to your batteries so it functions as a true ESV. The only disadvantage I see to a tach with a digital readout is that the display changes quite a bit as you get your reading. Craft-Air is producing a very good tachometer that allows you to tach an engine turning a three-blade prop. Ace RC makes the Tachmaster 2, a very good unit that you can buy in kit form or assembled. It has a meter with three ranges, so it's very accurate for measuring idle and top end. To calibrate it, you point it at a fluorescent light bulb and push the button. Nice!

For more on how to use a tachometer, see Chapters 7 and 8.

Other Useful Field Tools

You should carry an assortment of tools with you when you go flying—not *too* many, since major adjustments and repairs should be done at home, not on the field. But a set of screwdrivers and Allen wrenches is very useful. A four-way wrench such as the Fox and Du-Bro units is a must; one of these will tighten prop nuts, wheel hubs, and glow plugs.

If your model has a wing held on by bolts, make sure you have a screwdriver or Allen wrench of the appropriate size. Sonic-Tronics makes a very nice tool for wing bolts that stores the bolts in the handle.

If you use rubber bands to hold the wing on, a few precautions are advised. You should store them in a plastic bag; Ziploc bags are good for this. I prefer to use the bands once and throw them away, since they get stretched out and greasy. If you don't want to do this, then store the used rubber bands in a separate bag with some talcum powder in it to absorb the oil. If they get too stretched out, throw them away . . . they're a lot cheaper than replacing the plane.

I carry about six inches of spare fuel tubing. Sometimes an engine runs too lean for no obvious reason, and tinkering with the needle valve is no help. One thing to try is to replace the fuel line from the tank to the carb. A pinhole or crack in this fuel line can admit air to the carb and cause a lean run.

I have a small plastic box with spare screws, nuts, and bolts. This includes prop nuts, which are impossible to find after they come flying off.

Finally, I carry a small bottle of Pacer's After Run Oil in my field box. After a day's flying I always put some oil into the engine crankcase to help prevent rusted bearings. If the evening is a fine one and I'm not too tired, I'll do this on the field while cleaning up the planes.

WHERE TO FLY—COMMON COURTESY

The very best place to go flying is your club's flying field. You are in surroundings that were laid out especially for flying model airplanes, so you don't have to cope with obstructions. You're a safe distance from spectators, and some sort of crowd control is in effect to keep people from wandering out onto the runway when you're coming in deadstick. And you're surrounded by friendly, knowledgeable fellow fliers who will be ready to offer helpful advice, occasional doses of sarcastic wit, and maybe even a glow plug or some fuel.

If you're a beginner, you should find a club field. There are a lot of reasons, but the main one is that you'll be much less likely to hurt yourself or others if you're in the controlled environment of the club field. Alternatively, pick a *big* field—like 15 or 20 acres—clear of trees and power lines, and with no other people around. You can't watch your plane and everyone else at the same time!

If the pasture you want to fly in isn't your property, find the owner and get his permission. This bit of common courtesy will come in real handy when you want to fly there again. And you might just make a new friend.

I strongly recommend against flying radio-controlled model airplanes at public parks or school fields. For one thing, there may well be rules against it. Many school boards and park authorities, made super-cautious by today's uncomprehensible liability insurance situation, will ban any faintly risky activity from their property. It doesn't matter that model aviation has an outstanding safety record; they don't understand it, that whirling propeller looks dangerous, and they don't want to be sued.

Another good reason not to fly at the local park is crowd control. People young and old seem to come out of nowhere when you fire up a model engine. They're going to make you nervous, and justly so. I have crashed airplanes deliberately on two different occasions because people appeared after I took off and stood right in the middle of my approach pattern, watching me fly. In one case, my frantic waving to get out of the way was greeted with a friendly wave in return! Confronted with such stubbornness, I killed the engine and went into the weeds. Fortunately, my spectators strolled away at this point; if they had come over to start asking why I landed that way, I might have told them.

Overhead power lines are another hazard: Don't fly anywhere near them. Not only can they snag airplanes, knocking them out of the sky if you're lucky and capturing them if you're not, but they can sometimes cause radio interference. And if conditions are right, you might become a lightning rod. I've seen power flow to the wires of a control line airplane from overhead power lines a hundred feet away. There was a flash, and the lines glowed like the filament of a light bulb, then vanished. The pilot wasn't seriously hurt, but none of us ever thought we'd get zapped that far away from the power lines! Your transmitter antenna could be the same kind of lightning rod.

Never, but never, climb a power pole to receive a stuck airplane! It seems that every year there are reports of people killing themselves by trying to retrieve kites or similar flying objects from power lines. The power company will come and get it for free if you call them.

If your only alternative is to fly at an uncontrolled site, take along someone else. You will need them to control any spectators who might show up. There's also the fact that you could get hurt, and need someone else there to help deal with it. Club fields have first-aid kits, as well as other experienced people—another good reason to find that club first!

FIELD FREQUENCY PROCEDURES

When you fly at a club field, you abide by the club's rules. The most important rules you have to follow are the frequency control procedures. These rules are intended to keep people from causing interference and "shooting down" aircraft that are in the air. You don't want it to happen to you, and you don't want to do it to someone else, so check those frequency rules!

Frequency control procedures will vary from field to field, but the most important thing that they all have in common is this: *Never* switch on your transmitter, no matter how briefly, until you're sure that you have control of the frequency you're on! Even if you just flick the transmitter switch on and off, that could be the moment that someone else on your frequency is coming in for a landing, and you could flip him over or slam him into the ground. Check your transmitter before you arrive, so you can be sure you don't drive up with a transmitter that's switched on and radiating. Don't laugh; it's happened to me.

Frequency Control Systems

There are two basic frequency control systems in common use, with variations to suit the particular club's taste. In the first and most common system, there's a frequency board with pins attached to it, one for each frequency. These pins are often ordinary spring-type clothespins, with a piece of wood or plastic glued to them and painted or printed with the frequency they represent. Ace RC sells a set of stickers showing each frequency, just for making up these pins. Each pin is attached to the main board at a point that represents its frequency, in order, so you don't have to hunt for the frequency you want to use.

Before you switch on your transmitter, you go to the board and pick up the pin with the frequency you're on. You clip the pin to your transmitter antenna. While the pin is in your possession, the frequency is yours, and you can switch your system on and fly. If the pin isn't there, someone else is using your frequency.

Many club fields have little plastic pockets built into their frequency board at each point where a pin is attached. When you take the frequency pin, you leave your AMA license card in the pocket. This shows other people the name of the person using the frequency, and proves that you're an AMA

If your club is small, maybe you won't have a frequency board or a transmitter impound. This makes it more important to check with all the other fliers and find the ones who are on the same channels you are. Make sure you don't switch on your transmitter while they're flying on your channel!

member and covered by insurance. It also gives you a strong incentive not to forget to put the pin back and drive home with it still attached to your transmitter!

Most clubs employing this system have a rule about how long you can keep the frequency pin when someone else is waiting for it. Generally, you can fly as long as you like; but chores like tweaking the engine should be done at home where you're not holding up someone else who wants to fly. A little courtesy and understanding will go a long way.

The second frequency control system common at club fields works in the opposite way. Each club member comes to the field with a pin of his own that has his name on it. It also shows the frequency of his transmitter. When he wants to fly, he places his pin on the frequency board in the position that represents the frequency he uses. A glance at the board shows what frequencies are in use and who is using them.

This system isn't as common, mainly because of people like me who forget to bring their frequency pins with them! It also means that you have to make yourself another pin each time you buy a radio system tuned to a different frequency from the one you were using. But it does ensure that all fliers at a particular field are club members and know the rules. So some clubs with limited memberships use this system.

Frequency Flags

Most clubs require that you display your frequency with a flag attached to your transmitter antenna while you're flying. This makes it easier to determine which frequency you're using without having to come over and ask you while you're concentrating on your plane. You probably got a frequency flag with your radio when you bought it. If not, or if you lost yours, the radio manufacturer will usually sell you another one. Ace RC sells frequency flags that fit any antenna; you buy the two channel numbers you need, and a set of nylon straps and clips to attach it to your antenna.

Originally, radio control frequencies were designated by a two-color code. In the 72 megahertz (MHz) band where most people fly, one of these colors was white. So you would have a frequency flag that was brown and white, red and white, purple and white, etc. That was fine when we only had a few frequencies! Now that more frequencies have opened up, we've gone to a system of numbered channels. You can get more information on this in Chapter 3, where we go into the frequency scheme in detail. Suffice it to say that you'll have two numbers on your frequency flag that tell you (and everyone else) what channel you're flying on. Most people refer to the channel number rather than to the frequency, because it's easier to remember Channel 46 than 72.590 MHz.

FIELD COURTESY

Most club field rules come down to common courtesy and sense. For example, most clubs ask that you not run your engine up to full throttle in the pit area where everyone is setting up their own equipment. The noise is annoying, and if your spinner comes off or your prop sheds a blade, it could be dangerous. Take your plane out to an empty spot on the taxiway or at one end of the pit area and perform your preflight engine tests.

Taxi your airplane only in the areas designated for it. When your engine is running, that prop presents a safety hazard. If you're taxiing where people are standing, and the plane gets away from you for whatever reason, one of your friends could stop it with his leg. It's simpler and easier to carry the plane out of the pits to the beginning of the taxiway, and taxi it onto the field.

While we're on the subject, here is something else to think about while you're taxiing your plane. You should avoid taxiing in such a way that someone else with an active transmitter in their hands comes between you and the plane. Picture a line of pilots on the flight line, maybe four of them spaced 20 feet apart up and down the line. You should never taxi your plane in front of them, close in. If any of those transmitters is poorly tuned and splattering, it could make your receiver twitch as it gets closer to the bad transmitter. If it twitches your throttle channel, the plane can get away from you.

Takeoff Procedure

Stay close to your plane as you taxi out to the flight line. Stop short of the runway and check out the other folks in the air. Anyone who is on final approach to land has absolute right of way. Don't attempt to taxi out and take off before they get in. The pilot is concentrating on his airplane, setting up his approach, and following it through. Extend to him the same courtesy you want extended to you.

With your plane idling at the side of the runway, take up your position on the flight line. Check a final time to make sure no one is on approach. If you're not sure, ask. Now announce that you are taking off. Taxi out and turn into the wind. You're ready to go.

''On the Field!''

The runway is no place to stand at any time. Fliers can't keep one eye on their plane and the other on people milling around. The runway and the area on the other side of it where the planes are in the air are ''off limits'' when anyone is flying. It's a basic element of the AMA Safety Code; we never, never fly over peoples' heads.

Sometimes, though, you have to go out on the runway. You might have the engine flame out just as you were advancing the throttle for takeoff. (It's probably too lean; see Chapter 7.) You might have nosed over and hit the prop against the ground, or taxiied into the weeds at the edge of the runway. (Many fields leave these weeds tall, so they act as plane-catchers if you come in too fast and run out of runway.)

If you have to go out on the runway, make sure the other pilots know it. Announce ''On the field!'' in a loud voice. Get out there, get your plane, and get back as fast as you can. Don't run, but walk quickly. Don't try to restart the engine or check out the problem until you're out of the way.

As you leave the runway, announce ''All clear!'' The other pilots will know you're out of the way and they can get back to normal operations.

Flying Courteously

As you're flying, you'll find that there are some other basic rules to follow. Like the rest, they're based on the Golden Rule: Treat the other pilots as you would want them to treat you.

You're concentrating on your airplane. You can't take the time to watch out for everyone else. There's a lot of sky up there, and planes are relatively small. But midair collisions happen. The best way to avoid midairs is to fly conservatively. Save your hot-dog maneuvers for when you've got the field to yourself or there's only one other pilot up.

If your engine quits, announce ''Dead stick!'' right away. The other pilots will give you the right of way. If you are on final approach and someone calls ''Dead stick,'' add throttle and go around. If you've just landed or are getting ready to take off, taxi out of the way. The pilot with the dead stick plane will be concentrating completely on his plane. His options are limited, since his plane will lose altitude fast if he makes a sharp turn. Don't get in his way.

When you're ready to land, announce your intention. "Coming in!" or "On final!" are the common expressions. This gives you priority for landing, except in the event of a dead stick or similar emergency.

Speaking of emergencies, if you are having trouble, make sure the other pilots know it! If your plane is behaving in an unpredictable manner, for whatever reason, request the right of way by announcing, "I'm having trouble!" Reduce your throttle and land right away. The place to troubleshoot is on the ground, not in the air.

Chapter 7

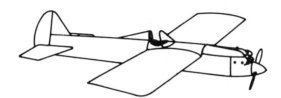

Two-Stroke Engines

MOST OF THE ENGINES USED IN MODEL AIRCRAFT are *two-strokes*. They have become popular because they're easy to handle, reliable, and inexpensive. Two-stroke engines do best at higher rpm, and generally deliver more usable power than four-strokes of the same displacement. Since they have fewer parts than four-strokes, they're easier to design and manufacture. With minimal care, they'll give you good service for many years.

ENGINE SAFETY

Statistically, when someone hurts themselves with a model airplane, it usually involves the engine. Most actual injuries involve the propeller. The only sure way to prevent accidents like this is to treat with great respect any running engine, no matter where it is or how big it is. Propellers are meant to cut air, not fingers, but they'll do an effective job of cutting fingers if you let it happen.

The basic rule to follow is simple: never under any circumstances, reach over the running prop. You have to be in front of the engine to start it. Once

it's started, the *first* thing you do is move around behind it. Of course, this means that your plane is being held in place, either by a friend (best) or a secure tiedown mechanism. If it makes you feel more comfortable, it's allowable to have your left hand around the fuselage of the airplane holding it in place while you start the engine. But remember, that arm is in danger! Remove it as quickly as possible. Don't disconnect the plug connector, or diddle with the needle valve; *get your arm out of the way!* Stand up, walk around behind the prop, and remove the glow plug connector. This is not only safer, it gives the engine a chance to warm up. Your needle valve adjustments will be far less tricky if you give the engine a chance to get up to operating temperature. It's also good exercise!

Be conscious of the prop arc. Picture the propeller on the front of the engine, level across the front of the plane. Visualize a straight line drawn from each propeller tip out a hundred feet or so. This line is the danger zone. Every now and then, a prop with a hairline crack you didn't notice will throw a

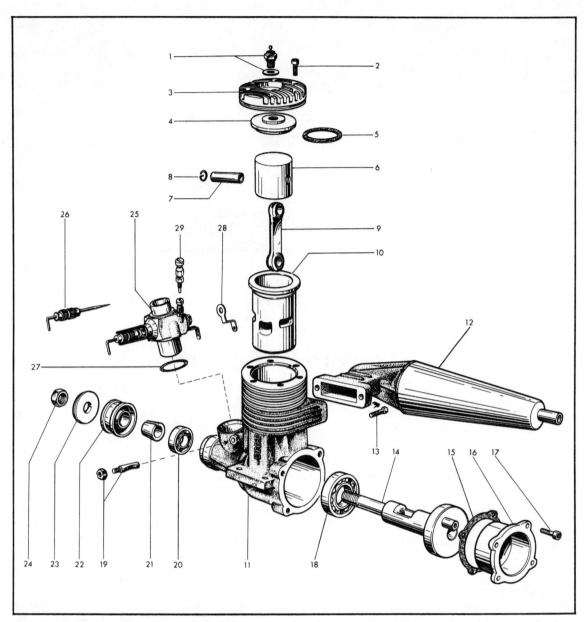

Two-stroke engines typically take in their fuel mixture through the hollow crankshaft, into the crankcase, and up the sides of the cylinder through ports in the cylinder or liner. Movement of the piston covers and uncovers the intake and exhaust ports. This drawing shows a Rossi .40 racing and sport engine. (Illustration courtesy MRC)

blade, or an over-rich engine will backfire and kick the prop loose. Heavy-handed application of the starter can loosen the prop nut, too. Don't let spectators stand to either side of the plane along the prop arc while the engine is running. Don't stand there yourself! Be aware of everything along that line and in front of it. Awareness is the key to safe flying.

CARBURETORS

You are likely to spend a lot of time tinkering

with carburetors, trying to find the magical combination of settings that will give you a first-flip start every time. But before you start tweaking, remember an important rule: The engine arrives from the factory preset where the manufacturer wants it. The carb is adjusted in a way that will make the vast majority of that particular engine run right. It will almost always work the way you want it, right out of the box. If adjustment is necessary, it should be very small amounts of it—just enough to adapt the engine to the conditions of air pressure and humidity at your flying field, and the nitro content of your favorite fuel.

Most (almost all) carburetors have the same adjustments on them. Let's look at these one by one.

Needle Valve

The main needle valve is the carb adjustment you'll spend the most time on. It meters the amount of fuel flowing into the carburetor. The needle valve is the main thing that determines how rich or lean the engine will run. See Chapter 6, Flying, for field procedures for properly adjusting your needle valve. When we discuss troubleshooting carbs, which we will do shortly, we'll go into how to clean needle valve assemblies.

Idle Adjustment

Carburetors have some sort of adjustment to allow you to control the fuel-air mixture at idling speed. Adjustments to the idle mix should not be done until the engine is broken in; see our comments on breaking engines in later in this chapter. The main needle valve should always be adjusted first, since changing the main needle will affect the idle setting. Get your top speed adjusted first, then go for a good idle.

There are two types of idle adjustment; most carbs have one or the other. The most common idle adjustment is simply a hole in the front or back of the carb body. A screw is threaded into a hole in the top of the carb that intersects with this hole. By turning the screw in, you can block off the hole. This "air bleed" is only functional when the carb throttle barrel is in the idle position; the sides of the carb

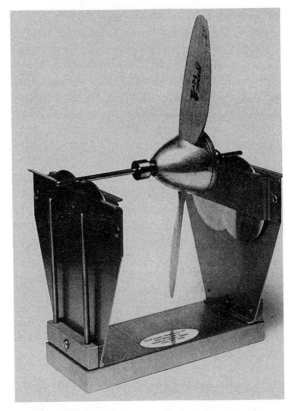

New props should always be balanced. Mounting them on a High Point Balancer like this one is one of the best ways to do it. Sand the back of the heavier blade until it doesn't fall to the bottom. (Photo by Jennifer Pratt)

barrel will block the hole when the throttle is advanced.

Adjusting the air bleed is simple and straightforward. Turning the screw in blocks off part of the air flowing in, making the engine idle richer. Turning the screw out leans the idle mixture.

This adjustment should be made a quarter turn at a time, no more. In practice, it is seldom necessary to adjust the air bleed. In any case, don't adjust the idle until after you've made a couple of break-in runs on the engine.

The other type of idle adjustment is a needle valve, just like the one that controls the fuel mix at high speed, but smaller. This is adjusted the same way that the air bleed screw described above is adjusted. It should be moved in very small increments—no more than a quarter turn at a time.

Throttle Stop

The typical throttle barrel has a groove cut in it. A screw projects through the top of the carb body into this groove. The throttle barrel rotates as far as the tip of the throttle stop screw will permit it.

Tightening this screw will limit the travel of the throttle barrel, making the engine idle at a higher rpm and achieve a slightly lower rpm at the top end. Conversely, loosening this screw will allow the barrel to travel slightly farther.

You almost never have to tinker with the throttle stop. If your engine is well broken-in and easy to run, and you want to try for a lower idle, it might be necessary to back the throttle stop out a quarter turn to let the barrel move farther. If you want to be able to shut the engine down by closing the throttle completely, and the engine will still run at the lowest throttle setting, try loosening the throttle stop slightly.

Your engine may incorporate adjustments that are slightly different from the ones I've described. Read the engine's instructions carefully.

Troubleshooting Carbs

If your engine won't run the way you want it to, the first place to look is the carburetor. Most engine problems, in my experience, are solved here.

If your plane is tail-heavy, the easiest way to correct it is to add weight to the nose. Harry's Heavy Hub, from Harry Higley & Sons, puts the weight in front of the prop, where it does the most good. Sizes are available for most engines. (Photo courtesy *Model Retailer* magazine)

Enya engines have a reputation for lasting a long time and producing plenty of power. This Enya SuperSport .40 is a good basic sport engine. It has an air bleed-type carburetor with an adjustable air inlet in the front. (Photo courtesy Altech Marketing)

Does the engine start, increase its speed, then stop abruptly? It's too lean. Turn the needle valve out a quarter turn and try again. If adjusting the needle valve doesn't help, something else is obstructing the fuel flow to the engine. Inspect the fuel line closely for hairline cracks that admit air. Bubbles in the fuel line are a sure sign of this.

If your engine is lean and adjusting the needle valve doesn't help, there may be dirt obstructing the carb. Fuel enters the carb past the needle valve into a small pipe called a *spraybar*. The spraybar has a slit in the side that the fuel sprays from, mixes with the incoming air, and so on into the motor. If particles of dirt block this slit and obstruct the fuel flow, you get lean runs.

To clear the carb, get a fuel squeeze bulb with a length of fuel tubing attached. Suck a little fuel into the bulb. Remove the needle valve, and fit the fuel tubing down over the threads that held the needle in place on the carb. Now give the bulb a hefty squeeze. This will spray fuel through the spraybar from the opposite direction at considerable pressure, and should dislodge any dirt particles. Invert the engine and flush out the carb with fuel from the bulb.

This sport .40 engine is made by Irvine Engines in England. Irvine engines feature carburetors with molded plastic bodies. They have a good reputation as solid, easy-running sport engines. (Photo courtesy *Model Retailer* magazine)

Now refit the needle valve to where it was before and try running the engine again.

You can avoid problems like this if you use fuel filters, both in the line from the fuel tank to the carburetor and also in the tubing going into your fuel pump. One of the places where dirt gets into the fuel is the fuel can, especially if you drop the cap onto the ground!

Check to be sure there are no air leaks in and around the carburetor. Is it firmly fitted into the crankcase housing? How about the fittings; are they tight? I had a problem with my K&B .20, which tended to go lean when the plane was in the air. I suspected an air leak, and dismounted the carb to inspect it. (This is very simple on K&B engines, by the way.) I plugged the fuel intake with my finger, attached a squeeze bulb to the needle valve inlet as described above, and squeezed a little air into it. I intended to clear any grit out of the carb jet, but I also noticed some bubbles coming out around the base of the fuel inlet where it screws into the cast carb body. A moment's work with a nut driver tightened it up, and my problem disappeared with the bubbles.

Avoiding Lean Runs

One thing that can seriously damage your engine is running it too lean. There's a danger zone with two-stroke engines where they will continue to run until they overheat, unlike four-strokes, which simply die if they're set too lean. Be aware of where

your needle valve is set; it should always be on the rich side.

A big mistake that many people make is assuming that since the needle is set correctly on the ground, it'll be set correctly in the air! Two things conspire to change the fuel mixture once the plane is airborne. First of all, the plane isn't level much of the time; it's turning, climbing, or diving. Gravity affects the fuel feed. If the plane's nose is pointing up, the engine works harder to draw fuel from the tank, and leans out. Secondly, when the prop is moving through the air, it doesn't require as much energy as it does when the plane is restrained on the ground. This is why you hear people referring to props ''unloading'' in the air. The engine will attain a higher rpm in the air than on the ground, and this can lead to a dangerously lean run.

The simple way to avoid this is to set the engine rich. Find the rpm peak on the ground, and back off the needle valve. Go through the procedure described in Chapter 6, Flying, where you hold the plane with its nose in the air. If the engine doesn't lean up in this attitude, you're safe to fly.

Learn to listen to your engine while the plane is in the air. If you leave it at a constant throttle setting, and tool around through a few turns, be alert to any change in engine speed. A sagging of rpm is a warning sign. If the engine slows down, especially while maneuvering, land and richen it up two clicks or so. If you pull the throttle stick back to idle, and you hear it idle fast for a second and slow down, land and richen it up. Remember: err on the rich side!

Webra engines are popular for their high speed and precisely adjustable carburetors. They offer a wide range of sizes, and special engines for helicopters and cars. Left to right: .61 side exhaust, .61 Long Stroke, and .61 Helicopter. (Photo courtesy *Model Retailer* magazine)

GLOW PLUGS

You'll find that glow plugs fall into two groups. "RC" plugs have a small bar that crosses the end of the plug, partially hiding the glow element itself. This is sometimes called an *idle bar*. "Standard" plugs have no such bar; the glow element is completely exposed.

Some engines don't require a plug with an idle bar. In fact, I seldom use them unless the engine's instructions specifically call for them. The purpose of the idle bar is to protect the glow element from direct sprays of fuel that will put it out. This can happen with certain engines at idle, where the ports that carry the fuel-air mix aim it up toward the top of the cylinder. Carburetors are designed to provide a rich fuel mix at idle. The idle bar helps protect the glow element when this rich mix comes in.

You will also hear of plugs referred to as "cool" or "hot." This refers to the fuel that the plug was designed to operate with. The higher the nitro content of the fuel, the colder the plug. Most sport flying plugs are warm, since most sport fliers seldom fly with fuel containing more than 15 percent nitro. Warm plugs have a wider tolerance to sport fuels.

MAINTENANCE

Maintaining a modern two-stroke engine is largely a matter of protecting it from things that can damage it. When it comes to disassembling the engine, my rule is *don't take an engine apart unless there's no other choice!* This applies most emphatically to the cylinder, piston and sleeve. No matter how careful you are in removing a sleeve from a cylinder, it isn't going to go back in the same way. This can mean that you have to break in the engine all over again (at best). I'm comfortable with removing the backplate on the back of the crankcase; this is often useful to see if there's any metal flashing around the edges of the crankcase casting. Removing the backplate will help you determine if you have a bent connecting rod or crankpin, or if the bearing surfaces of the rod and pin are worn. If you're having trouble with an engine and removing the backplate doesn't reveal the problem, send it back to the manufacturer for service.

What Can Ruin an Engine? The fuel we use is mostly alcohol, which is hygroscopic. This means that it attracts water from the atmosphere. A puddle of fuel in the crankcase or around the bearings of your engine will cause rust in a distressingly short time. Furthermore, some additives put in fuel to improve ignition also attract moisture.

The best way to make sure there's no fuel left in your engine at the end of the day is to run it dry. With the throttle set at idle, pull the fuel line off the carburetor inlet. The engine will speed up as it leans out, and quit. Now hook your glow plug battery up to the plug and flip the prop. You might get a pop or two as the last of the fuel vapor is pulled into the

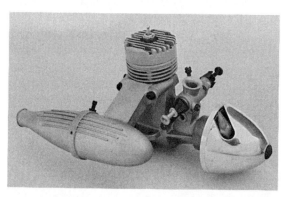

The new Fox .40 BB Deluxe is an outstanding sport .40 engine. It comes with muffler and a polished aluminum spinner. The new-style carburetor has separate needle valves for idle and full speed adjustment. (Photo courtesy Fox Manufacturing)

The Fox Eagle .60 is recognized as one of the most powerful .60 engines available. The tuned exhaust pipe shown will add considerably to the engine's speed, and is very quiet. (Photo courtesy Fox Manufacturing)

cylinder. When the popping stops, remove the battery; you've dried out the engine. This simple procedure will do more to make your engines live a long time than anything else.

Castor oil is a rust inhibitor. So if you are using a fuel with some castor oil in the mix, such as Sig, K&B, Red Max, and others, you are less likely to get rust. Some of these fuels also include rust inhibitors, but I have the most faith in castor oil.

What If You Have a Lean Run? Sometimes you'll find yourself with an overheated engine, for any of the reasons we've talked about. The way you handle it can make the difference between ruining your engine and simply learning a lesson!

If you hear the engine leaning out in the air, land at once. Don't kill the engine unless you have to. Once you have it on the ground, richen the engine by about a quarter turn of the needle valve. Let it cool off at idle speed. If you simply shut off an overheated engine, it can warp. The piston ring can lose its temper, or several other nasty things could happen. The unburned fuel and oil moving through the engine as it idles rich will cool it quickly and consistently. Since most carbs are set to richen the mixture automatically, if you idle the engine and glide in for a landing, it should be safely cool by the time you get it down.

STARTERS

A starter is a good investment. It'll save you a lot of time and grief on the flying field. Of course, as a general rule, the engine should start by simply flipping the prop with a chicken stick (remember: *never* with your finger!). But a starter will simplify the whole process of starting, since it won't be necessary to prime or choke the engine. (More on this later.)

The standard starters are made by Sullivan. There are several different sizes, depending on how large an engine they will be used for. You can also buy different shaped cones for the front end of the starters, to fit starting connections on helicopters, boats, and ducted fan engines. I've gotten along just fine with the least expensive Sullivan starter, which has handled everything from .09 to 2.40 engines for me.

The K&B .40, one of the most widely-used engines in the world. This classic American engine has been updated with a new carburetor that is easier to adjust. It's a fine performer that never seems to wear out. (Photo courtesy K&B Manufacturing)

There are other brands of starters available, many of them for lower prices than the Sullivan starter. You could save a few bucks with some of these, but don't expect them to last as long as a name brand unit like the Sullivan. One other starter I've used with very good success is made by Kavan in Germany and imported by several different retailers. This has a relatively small motor, and a planetary gear arrangement in the head to provide lots of torque to the cone on the front.

A company called Neu Kraft has released an interesting new starter called a Bump Start. It looks like a standard starter, but instead of an electric motor it contains a powerful spring. Wind it backwards a few turns, and a ratchet holds it in place. Place the cone against the engine spinner and push forward hard enough to release the ratchet. The spring turns your engine over. It's a very nice product, capable of starting most standard motors. And you don't have to lug around a 12-volt battery to power it!

Starter Cautions. There are several things that you should be aware of when you use a starter. First and foremost, if your engine is even slightly

This remarkable outboard motor system for RC boats was designed by K&B's engine wizard Bill Wisniewski. Cooling water is ducted in the front, around the cylinder head, and out the back. The engine exhausts into an integral muffler that vents underwater. The whole business mounts on a pivot for steering. (Photo courtesy K&B Manufacturing)

flooded, turning it over with a starter can damage it. I don't prime or choke an engine before applying a starter to it. I always flip the prop over a few times by hand before applying the starter. If it starts without it, fine. If it doesn't, I'm certain it's not flooded. Cranking a flooded engine with a starter can bend the wristpin or connecting rod. You'll wonder why the engine just doesn't seem to have the performance it once did. If your piston didn't go all the way to the top, you wouldn't perform well either!

Occasionally you'll see "experts" at the flying field smack their starter against the engine spinner, bumping the engine to life, or they lean into it, putting lots of pressure on the starter. I cringe when I see this, because I know what's happening inside the engine. The crankshaft is being jammed up tight

against the backplate of the engine. Metal is being scraped off the backplate. I've seen backplates that have had deep slots milled into them by this kind of treatment. Where do you think that metal goes? Right through the engine, scoring and scratching the piston and cylinder liner as it goes.

You should never have to jam the starter cone up against the engine spinner to turn the engine over. You should be able to hold it firmly in contact and push the starter switch to turn the engine over easily. If it takes more, you either have a flooded engine or a nearly flat starter battery. Check both possibilities before trying the starter again.

FUEL

Glow fuel consists of three major components: *alcohol* (methanol, to be exact), *nitromethane*, and *lubricant*. Manufacturers also mix in small quantities of other components: ignition aids, detergents, rust inhibitors, and so on.

The alcohol is the major component. It reacts catalytically with the hot platinum element in the glow plug to keep the engine running. The nitromethane assists this process; that's why higher nitro contents improve the high-end rpm and idle performance of the engine. The oil isn't just along for the ride; without it, the engine would rapidly overheat and seize up, just as your car engine would.

When you buy fuel for your sport models, you should have two considerations in mind. The first is the amount of nitro that you need. Almost all of

The new K&B .20 Sportster engine was an instant hit. The engine has no bearings or bushings; advanced metallurgy makes them unnecessary. The .20 is supremely easy to run, and thanks to an advanced muffler design, is very quiet in the air. A larger Sportster engine, the K&B .45, has just become available. (Photo courtesy K&B Manufacturing)

The Royal .40 has become very popular as a sport engine in the last few years. It's inexpensive, and very easy to adjust and run. The Royal .40 can even by used in racing events. (Photo courtesy *Model Retailer* magazine)

the engines used in sport models today in the U.S. will run very happily on 10 to 15 percent nitro fuel. Unless you're racing, there's no need for more. Many engines, particularly Fox engines, will run cheerfully on 5 percent nitro fuel. Nitro is expensive, so the smaller the nitro content, the cheaper the fuel.

Experimentation will quickly tell you what nitro percentage a particular engine likes. Try a tankful of fuel on the ground. Run the engine all the way up to full throttle. Is the needle valve adjustment easy to find, or does a few clicks either way make the difference between smooth running and stopping? Higher nitro content is called for if the needle is hard to set. Now move the throttle to idle. Poor idling is another sign that the engine wants more nitro. Finally, move the throttle from idle to wide open. Does the engine bog down for a second before it picks up speed? This could be a result of poor needle valve adjustment, but if you've been tinkering with the needle and everything else is fine, higher nitro content might solve this.

The other consideration in buying sport fuel is the lubricant. Synthetic oils are cheaper than castor oil, and the cheaper sport fuels don't have castor

in them. I like castor oil in my fuel. There are several reasons why I don't mind cleaning off the unburned castor that comes out my muffler, but there are two in particular. First, castor oil is better at carrying away heat from the engine than any of the commonly used synthetic lubricants. This is because castor oil has a higher "flashpoint" and doesn't burn (or burns very little) at running temperatures. Second—and most important—castor oil inhibits rust. Both of these things will help your engine live a long, happy life.

You'll hear many different opinions about the relative value of different brands of fuel. Here are mine; please take them as *opinions* and not definitive rules. I have had very good success with K&B and SIG fuel, and I use one or the other of these brands to break in new engines. I know there's plenty of castor in the mix to help new engines run cool and slick. For everyday flying, I use Red Max and Cool Power fuels—good, inexpensive stuff. JMD fuel is excellent for more sensitive engines; I especially like their four-stroke mix.

When I hit the hobby shop for fuel, I read the labels carefully. If they say there's castor oil in the lubricant mix, I'll try the fuel. If not, I ask others who are using it for their opinions. As with most of the other things I buy, I'm suspicious of the cheapest can on the shelf. I'd rather spend three or four "ex-

This Como .40 is made in Italy by Super Tigre; the Como engines are almost identical to Super Tigres. The .40 is a powerhouse, and remarkably easy to start and run. Como engines are available from Indy RC and World Engines. (Photo by Jennifer Pratt)

tra'' bucks on a gallon of fuel than burn up a $100 engine!

TEST STANDS

You will need a test stand to run your engines on before you put them in your plane. True, you can break in the engine while it's mounted in the plane; you'll probably do this on your first plane. But it's very inconvenient to hold onto the plane through half an hour of running. It makes a lot more sense to have a test stand where you can quickly bolt the engine in place and run it without getting a backache.

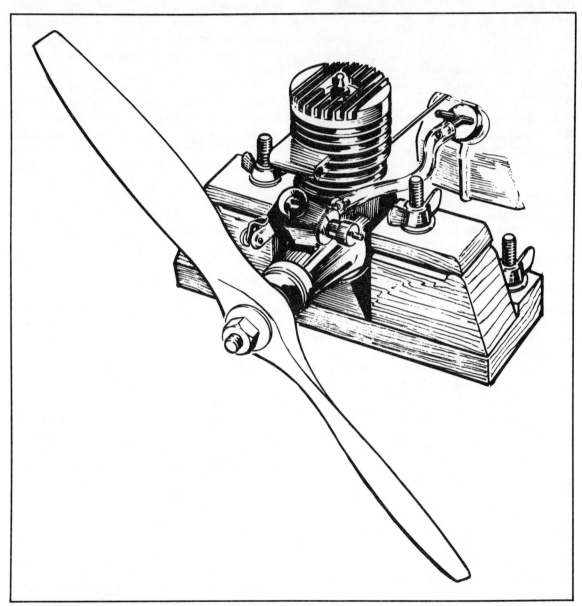

An engine test stand is essential for testing and breaking in new engines. This hardwood test stand from Carl Goldberg Models can be easily mounted to a bench or sawhorse. Aluminum test stands for larger engines are made by J'Tec and Tatone Products. (Illustration courtesy Carl Goldberg Models)

Several manufacturers sell special engine mounts for test stands. Carl Goldberg Models sells one that's made from hard maple, and clamps down on the engine with two wing nuts. It's good for engines up to .60 size, but I want something that holds the engine more securely for engines larger than this. A cast aluminum mount is the answer. These are made by J'Tec and Tatone. One of these mounts will hold any engine you care to put in it.

If you have an old wooden picnic table, you could mount your test stand on one corner. I built a sawhorse with extra-long legs, since I'm a large person. It's five feet long, which is longer than it has to be, but makes it very solid. The engine mount is mounted on a crosspiece at one end. Behind the mount, on a block, is a fuel tank. The tank rests on a block to bring it up to the level of the carburetor, where it would be when installed in an airplane. A piece of wire with a clevis on the end, held in place with two staples, gives me throttle control. That's really all you need.

Tatone Products has come out with a new test stand that has a built-in gauge and spring. The engine mount slides in a small track, and is held back by the spring. You can lock it in place with a lever. Once your engine is running, you release the lock and throttle the engine up to full power. The gauge measures the amount of thrust the engine is putting out. It's calibrated on a scale of one to ten, so instead of getting foot-pounds of thrust out of it, you use it to make comparisons. You can test different props on the same engine and see for yourself how much static thrust they produce. This is an excellent way to get a feel for the correct size prop that a particular engine will require.

BREAKING-IN TWO-STROKE ENGINES

No new engine is going to develop its full power or its smoothest idle right out of the box. An engine's running characteristics are heavily dependent on the fit of several parts, most of which are in metal-to-metal contact. The most obvious example of this is the fit between the sides of the piston and the walls of the cylinder or liner. That engine you just took out of the box was assembled from parts that were machined to very close tolerances. They will finish the job by machining themselves to a precise fit with each other during the first hour or so of running. This is the process called *breaking in.*

Breaking in an engine is not a complicated procedure. First of all, read the instructions! This may sound like an obvious point, but I keep harping on it because people don't do it. If your engine has special requirements during break-in, the manufacturer will know about it and tell you.

The object of breaking in is to bring your engine up to operating temperature and speed, but slowly, and without allowing the engine to overheat. Running the engine rich is a sure way to keep the engine from overheating, since the unburned fuel and oil carry away much of the heat produced by combustion. The oil cleans, cools, and lubricates the engine. The extra oil also has the effect of carrying away metal that is machined away during the break-in process. This is why you'll often see black gunk in the exhaust of a brand-new engine; that's metal powder from the final machining process as the parts rub together.

My usual procedure is to set up the engine on my test stand, and put on a prop one inch smaller in diameter than the size recommended for normal running conditions. This loads the engine more lightly, simulating the higher rpm the engine will achieve when it ''unloads'' in the air. I use 10 percent nitro fuel for break-in, since it's cheap and readily available. I always use a fuel with castor oil in the lubricant mix, such as SIG or K&B. Fox Super Fuel has more castor oil than any other commercial blend. Castor oil has much better heat transfer properties than other lubricants found in model fuel.

I set the needle valve where the instructions say for the first start. This can be anywhere from 2½ to 4 turns out from the fully closed position. I choke the engine, advancing the throttle to full open and hold my finger over the carb inlet until I can see that fuel has been drawn all the way into the carb. After choking, I pull the prop through a few more times. This helps to vaporize the fuel that's in the crankcase, and assures me that I haven't got a flooded engine. Now I reduce the throttle to half or a little above. Finally, I connect the glow plug battery and pull the prop through again. When the battery is connected to the plug, I hold the prop firmly between my thumb and forefinger; I never flip it through with my finger. If the charge of fuel and air in the cylinder is just right, I'll feel a bump as the charge ignites. If that bump is there, I know everything's ready, and I flip the prop with my chicken stick.

AAC OR ABC?

You will see different engines described as being "ABC" or "AAC." This refers to the cylinder and piston construction of the engine. *ABC* means that the piston is *aluminum,* and it runs in a *brass* cylinder liner that is *chromed* on its inner surface. *AAC* means that the piston is *aluminum*, the cylinder is *aluminum,* and the cylinder wall is *chromed.* Most recently designed sport engines are AAC.

There is little practical difference between the two. ABC engines tend to produce a bit more power. The cylinders are also designed so that the cylinder is just slightly narrower at the head than it is at the bottom. This improves compression, because the liner expands as the engine warms up and would move away from the piston if it wasn't tapered like this. It means that ABC engines need to be at or near their normal operating temperature while running, so the brass liner will be expanded to the proper shape. So, while breaking in an ABC engine, don't run it slobbering rich; a half turn from the highest speed setting is adequate for the first 30 minutes of running.

AAC engines are not as critical. Since the piston and cylinder are both made of the same material, they both expand at the same rate. Break these engines in as rich as they'll run for the first five minutes of running, then lean them out gradually over 30 minutes as we've described earlier.

LAPPED OR RINGED?

You will also see some engines referred to as "lapped" rather than "ringed." This refers to the way the piston is fitted to the cylinder or cylinder liner. A ringed engine has piston rings that form a seal between the piston and the cylinder wall. A lapped engine has a piston that has been honed or lapped to a near-perfect fit with the cylinder.

In practical terms, there isn't much difference between the two. Lapped engines take longer to break in, since there's considerably more surface area that has to wear to fit. Once thoroughly broken in, lapped engines tend to last forever. But there's no real reason to prefer one kind over the other.

ENGINE MAINTENANCE

The most important maintenance you can do on any engine is to run it dry at the end of a day's flying. We've discussed this earlier; all you have to do is remove or pinch off the fuel line and let the engine run until it stops. Then connect your glow plug battery and flip the prop until the engine doesn't pop. This makes sure that there's no fuel left in the engine; since the fuel attracts moisture from the air, leftover fuel will rust your engine's innards.

If the plane is going to be stored for any length of time such as over the winter, I'll put a few drops of oil into the carburetor and flip the prop to distribute it through the crankcase. Then I'll remove the plug, inject a few more drops into the cylinder through the plug hole, and turn the engine over some more.

The oil I use for this is Marvel Mystery Oil, the penetrating kind. Pacer Technology sells After Run Oil that works very well for the purpose too; in fact, it penetrates a little better. You could use 3-in-1 oil, but it tends to dry out and leave gunk inside the engine. FHS Supply, the Red Max Fuel people, also make an after run oil that's very good for this.

When you hang up the plane for the winter, don't hang it nose-down. Any unburned fuel in the muffler will run back down into the engine and finally wind up in the front bearings. Hang it with the nose pointing up, or horizontally.

ENGINE REPAIR

Unless you're a machinist, I suggest leaving major engine repairs to experts. The most I ever do to an engine is remove the backplate and inspect it for metal flak or grit. I flush out the crankcase with kerosene, and oil the bearings.

Removing the backplate isn't going to change

any of the bearing surfaces or tolerances of the engine. Removing the head is relatively safe, as long as you take care to tighten it back down evenly. Tightening one screw all the way down before the others can distort the head. I almost never remove the piston or cylinder liner. It's just too difficult to get them back in the way they were. A well-broken-in engine will have a cylinder-to-piston fit that is perfect down to the crystalline structure of the metal. You can't hope to duplicate that fit again if you remove the piston.

If you suspect that one of the bearings in your engine is bad, or that the connecting rod or wrist pin is deformed, send the engine back to the manufacturer for service. They will be able to discover and fix the problem a lot faster than you will, and they have the parts handy.

DIESELS

For some reason, Diesel engines have never been as popular in this country as they have been in Europe. I'll never figure it out..I love 'em. The fuel is no more expensive than glow fuel (though it is smellier); the engines don't cost any more, they're perfectly easy to start, and you don't have to lug a battery around for the glow plug . . . or glow plugs, for that matter.

I will admit that Diesels put out a lot of exhaust—smoky, oily, pungent exhaust at that. But with a little care and planning, the exhaust can be ducted away from the plane, and you even get a muffling effect from the exhaust pipe as a bonus.

Diesels will swing a larger prop than a glow engine of the same displacement. They also accept a much wider range of props than two-stroke glow en-

This tiny Diesel was made by a Czechoslovakian machinist named Pfeffer. It's a gem: .036 displacement, with the tiniest RC carburetor I've ever seen. A few of these are still available from Carlson Engine Imports. (Photo by Jennifer Pratt)

gines. My PAW .29 Diesel runs best on a 12-6 (a glow engine of the same size would be using a 9-6), but will handle props from 9-4 to 14-5! The secret is the compression adjustment, which effectively gives you a method of regulating the ignition point.

Diesels idle better; there's no hot glow plug to cool off when the rpm gets too low. The above-mentioned PAW .29 will idle that 12-6 reliably at 1500 rpm. They're generally quieter than the corresponding two-stroke glow engines. With these virtues, why haven't they caught on?

Maybe it's because people are intimidated at having to set the compression screw in the head of the engine as well as the needle valve on the intake. This *can* be tricky at first, but once you find the right setting you'll seldom touch the compression lever again. Let me describe the technique I use on a Diesel engine to find the right setting.

Starting Diesels

I start out with a needle setting that I know is rich, three to four full turns open. If the engine starts with the needle too rich, it'll blubber for a while and give me a chance to lean it out. Then I choke the engine until it's almost flooded. This way I'm sure I'm not cranking a dry engine. You can tell when you've overdone it and flooded the engine when you can barely turn the prop over compression. When that happens, flip the prop back and forth (without pulling it all the way through) until you have forced enough raw fuel out through the ports to allow you to flip it over. Don't force it through compression! Diesel engines are beefier than glow engines, but you can still bend their crank pins.

Once you have the engine wet, start flipping the prop. I never use an electric starter on a Diesel. With the needle valve open wide, spinning the engine with an electric starter will draw more fuel in and can cause a hydraulic lock. Hand-flipping with a chicken stick will allow you to feel when the engine is getting ready to start. You can flip it with your finger, but use a finger protector such as the thick rubber one sold by Ace RC. Never flip any engine with an unprotected finger!

Flip it a few times to vaporize the fuel in the engine. If you hear a pop, or the prop stops abruptly

before going over compression, you're close to the point of ignition; keep flipping. If you've gotten no action at all, turn the compression screw in a quarter turn and flip some more. Turn the screw in until the engine starts to pop. It will, sooner or later.

Once you have the engine popping, it shouldn't take more than three or four flips to get it running. If it's still hesitant to light off, go in one-eighth turn on the compression screw.

Once the engine starts to run, be ready to back out the compression screw at least a half a turn. As the engine warms up, you require less compression for smooth running.

You should now be getting brief rich runs when you flip the prop. Go in on the needle valve a quarter turn at a time until the engine keeps running. At this point, a little tinkering with the compression and needle will give you consistent runs.

To start it up again, choke and flip. It may be necessary to turn the compression screw in a quarter turn when starting cold, especially on a chilly day. Back off the screw when the engine starts running. From here on, only minor adjustments of the compression screw will be necessary.

Breaking-In Diesels

Diesel engines require the same kind of break-in that regular two-strokes do. Similar rules apply. An engine with piston rings will break in more quickly than one with a piston that is lapped (fitted) directly to the cylinder.

I like to give new Diesels a good hour of bench running for break-in. It isn't necessary, but it helps familiarize me with the engine. I can play with different combinations of needle valve positions, compression settings, and props. By the time the engine goes in a plane, I know just how to make it behave.

Diesel Fuel

You can buy Diesel fuel from several different sources, or you can make your own. I've done both, but I prefer to buy it; it's a lot less trouble, and cheaper in the long run. To mix your own fuel, you need high-grade kerosene, castor oil, and ether. Kerosene is readily available; I buy it by the gallon for the little heater in my workshop. Castor oil is a little more difficult, but not much; SIG sells it by the gallon, and you can often get it at medical supply houses or drugstores. The ether is the problem. In some states you can't buy it over the counter without a prescription, because of its well-known anaesthetic qualities.

I've bought Diesel fuel from FHS Supply (makers of Red Max glow fuels) and Davis Diesel Development. Red Max diesel is available from stock, or on a custom order basis. If you're running small Diesels under .09 size, ask for more ether in the fuel mix to aid ignition. I buy fuel from FHS in gallons, but they very kindly package it in quart cans for me. This means I only have to open it as I need it. Since the ether evaporates very rapidly, this is a big advantage. Finally, Red Max Diesel fuel costs the same as their standard 10 percent nitro glow fuel.

Davis Diesel's fuel is excellent. They are Diesel experts, and are responsible more than anyone else for championing the Diesel cause in America. Davis fuel is available in two grades, one for engines smaller than .09 size, and one for larger engines. They will also provide special fuel for other applications. Davis sells a Diesel Concentrate, which you simply add to kerosene or lamp oil to get excellent fuel.

Eric Clutton, one of the importers of the popular P.A.W. Diesels, is now selling P.A.W.'s fuel in the U.S. Again, two grades are available, one for small engines and one for larger engines. Fuel coming straight from the engine manufacturer is hard to beat.

Where to Buy Diesels

Diesel engines can be hard to find. Not many hobby shops have them sitting around. Some stores will carry Davis Diesel's special replacement heads for standard two-stroke engines to convert them to Diesels. More about these later. But if you want a pure Diesel engine, you'll probably have to look for mail order sources. Model magazine ads are the best place to start looking.

I've bought Diesels from two small importers who specialize in them: Eric Clutton and Carlson En-gine Imports. Both have given me very fast service and friendly advice when I had questions.

Eric Clutton specializes in the P.A.W. line of Diesels from England. These are some of the most popular Diesels in Europe, and I've never seen anything that argues with that reputation.

Carlson imports P.A.W., and also has several other lines of interesting engines. They have the splendid reproduction Taplin Twin, an in-line twin cylinder Diesel. Carlson imports the Aurora diesels, and is a source for reproductions of the famous old Mills Diesels. When you send a buck to Carlson for his catalog, you'll get a list of rare and limited-supply engines that they have handy. At this writing, they still have some of the tiny .036 Pfeffer Specials for sale.

Dieselizing Glow Engines

Most Diesel fliers in the U.S. are doing it with glow engines that have been converted to Diesel. Conversion kits are made by Davis Diesel Development; as of now, there are over 120 different engines, and more are continually being developed. Dieselizing a glow engine will give you all the virtues of Diesel power with very little effort. Davis offers conversions for engines from the ubiquitous Cox .049 to the big Tartan and Supertigre 3000 engines. A dollar will bring you the current list and a lot of other good info besides.

A conversion kit consists of a new head for the engine cylinder. You remove the bolts holding on the glow head, being careful not to displace the gasket, and bolt on the Diesel head. Now you replace all of your fuel tubing in the plane with tubing that will stand up to Diesel fuel. Ordinary glow fuel line will swell up and relax when subjected to Diesel fuel. You may also have to replace the stopper in the fuel tank; DuBro sells replacement stoppers for gasoline and Diesel fuel.

That's all there is to it! The conversion head comes from the factory properly set for starting. Put on an appropriate prop, and start the engine the same way you would start any Diesel. The Davis instructions go into different starting methods in detail; read them first.

You'll get substantially more usable power from

This Cox .049 engine has been converted to run on Diesel fuel. The knurled knob on top of the head adjusts the compression. Dieselized engines can turn much bigger props. Davis Diesel Development sells the modification kit. (Photo by Jennifer Pratt)

a Dieselized engine. Planes that flew with a glow .40 can fly with a .25 or .30 Diesel. Diesels run much cooler than glow engines, so if your engine is inside a cowl, consider Dieselizing it. Finally, Dieselized engines run much quieter. You'll enjoy the difference!

Chapter 8

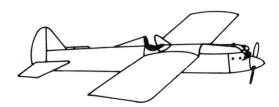

Four-Stroke Engines

FOUR-STROKE ENGINES WERE A CURIOSITY A FEW short years ago. Now they're all over the place. I've heard it said that their popularity is due to their sound, which is more like the rumble of a full-size aero engine than the whine of a two-stroke. Others say that they're the greatest for scale models, because they swing bigger props than two-strokes. I personally think that the extra mechanical parts appeal to those of us who love miniature machinery.

For whatever reason, four-strokes are here to stay. There are kits, fuels, engine mounts, and mufflers especially for them. New ones are being introduced all the time, and old ones are upgraded. Four-strokes have added a new dimension of pleasure to our sport.

RELATIVE POWER

Four-strokes deliver less power for their size than two-strokes. This is less true than it was when four-strokes were new. For the purposes of kit selection, to substitute a four-stroke engine for a two-stroke, go up one size. If the kit is designed for a two-stroke .60, consider a four-stroke .80 or .90. Kits intended for two-stroke .40 engines can be powered by four-stroke .60s. As with any general rule like this, it depends on the plane; a light plane, or one with plenty of wing, can use a smaller engine. Most of the kits we fly today are overpowered.

PROPS

Four-stroke engines are capable of turning larger, deeper-pitched propellers than two-strokes. This is because they develop their maximum usable power at lower rpm than two-strokes. The practical upshot of this is that, generally, a four-stroke will give you a slower-flying plane with a larger range of speeds.

You can start experimenting with the propeller you use for your four-stroke by trying a prop one size larger. Consult the engine instructions, and find the recommended rpm range. Mount the prop, start the engine, and tune the needle valve for peak performance as described later in this chapter. Now determine the maximum rpm with a tachometer. Go to idle, and make a note of how low an idle rpm you can get with no danger of the engine flaming out. Repeat this procedure with a prop an inch bigger, or an inch deeper in pitch. Now fly the plane with both props, looking for variations in performance. How fast does it get off the ground? Is the vertical performance affected? How about inverted flight? When you slow down for landing, does the plane sink or float differently? This is the kind of tinkering that will allow you to dial in your plane to where you like it. As you try this, you may even begin to notice differences between the brands of the same size prop.

Larger props have another beneficial effect. Since the large prop acts as a flywheel, a larger prop will almost always allow the engine to idle at a lower rpm. Heavier props have a similar effect. The special four-stroke props made by Master Airscrew and Dynathrust out of glass-reinforced plastic will show this effect. I fitted a Dynathrust 14-6 prop to my Saito .90, and was immediately able to idle it down another 300 rpm. It'll tick over at 2200 rpm with no risk of dying.

PROP KICKING

Some four-strokes have gotten a reputation for suddenly kicking the prop loose. This is almost always a result of running the engine too lean. Remember, you can't tune a four-stroke engine by ear the way you can a two-stroke. Use a tachometer, and look for the maximum rpm. When you find it, back off the needle valve a quarter turn at least. Since the engine will lean out in the air, you must set it rich on the ground.

Some fliers have recommended drilling and pinning props used on some of the larger four-strokes. To do this, two pins are inserted in the prop drive washer, immediately behind the prop hub. Two holes are drilled into the prop hub, and when the prop is put on the shaft, the pins go into the holes. If the engine kicks backward, the prop can't spin on the hub and loosen the prop nut.

I don't recommend this practice. Weakening the prop hub by drilling holes in it doesn't seem like a good idea to me. If an engine of mine has a tendency to loosen the prop, I might install a locknut on the shaft in place of the prop nut that came with the engine, but even this is seldom necessary. I've had my share of props loosened on starting (or trying to start) a four-stroke engine, and it was always because the engine was set wrong.

Think about it: Backfiring takes place because the fuel ignites too soon, while the piston is still on its way up. If the fuel mixture was correct, this wouldn't happen.

What do you do if your engine tends to kick its prop loose? Is it happening when you flip the prop to start it? The engine is probably flooded; don't choke it as much next time, or use an electric starter without priming or choking. Does it run for a while, and then stop and kick the prop loose? It's too lean; the excessive heat buildup is causing pre-ignition. Does it run fine at full throttle, but slow down and kick loose when you set the throttle to idle? Your idle is too lean; richen the idle adjustment.

ENGINE MOUNTS

Four-stroke engines are longer than two-strokes, because of the extra length of the crankshaft to hold the gears that drive the valves. Also, the carburetor is usually mounted out on the back of the engine, to bring it in line with the fuel tank. All this adds up to the need for a special engine mount.

There are two types of engine mounts you will find in your hobby shop. One is made of molded nylon, reinforced with glass fibers. Nylon engine mounts are strong, light, and flexible. They're very good for most purposes. When you buy one, make sure the arms fit your engine without having to be spread apart. Take your engine with you to the store and check.

The other type of engine mount is cast aluminum. These are heavier and more expensive than the nylon type, but they have several advantages. They are very rigid and will hold the engine tightly. They are drilled and tapped for your particular engine, and most come with bolts that fit the mounting holes. I've used quite a few aluminum engine mounts made by J'Tec and have been very satisfied with them. Tatone Products mounts are also excellent.

Edson Enterprises makes a unique series of cast aluminum engine mounts. They are each designed to accept a wide range of engines without being removed from the firewall. The arms of the mount fit in slots and are bolted in place. The mounting bolts fit in slots in the arms so they can accommodate different lengths of engines. It's a handy setup.

MUFFLERS

Because four-stroke engines produce a lower exhaust note than two-strokes, mufflers aren't an automatic requirement. However, as four-strokes became bigger and more powerful, they also got louder. Now most four-strokes either come with a muffler or have one available as an option.

I strongly recommend using the muffler if one is available for your engine. You can never be too quiet, after all. The muffler will often give you an outlet to pressurize your fuel tank as a bonus. This will make it easier to find a good needle setting.

GLOW PLUGS

Glow engines work on the principle that the engine retains enough heat to keep the plug element glowing brightly. This is what does the actual work of igniting the fuel. In four-stroke engines this is more difficult, since ignition only occurs every *other* time the piston reaches the top of the cylinder. So the engine manufacturer will often recommend a special glow plug that is better at retaining heat than the standard two-stroke plug.

O.S. was the first company to come out with a special four-stroke plug. While Saito and Enya engines would run fine with a standard plug, the O.S. four-strokes really liked their special plug. And the O.S. plugs would markedly improve the other brands. The only drawback was the the O.S. four-stroke plugs were quite expensive—as much as $5 apiece.

Now that four-strokes are more popular, special plugs are available for them that are a lot cheaper. The O.S. four-stroke plugs have come down in price. Sonic-Tronics has an excellent line of four-stroke plugs for all common brands. And Fox has just come out with a super plug that will improve the idle of any engine you use it in, especially a four-stroke. I bought a bucketful of the new Fox plugs when they came out, and I'm very pleased with the results.

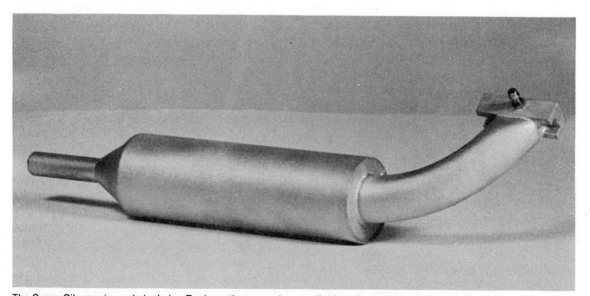

The Super Silencer is made by Irvine Engines; there are sizes available to fit many common engines. It does an excellent job of quieting the engine, and also provides a tuning effect that noticeably increases top-end rpm. (Photo courtesy *Model Retailer* magazine)

ADJUSTING THE CARBURETOR

Most carburetors on four-stroke engines are identical to the ones on two-stroke engines—at least on the outside. They are different on the inside, but the adjustments that we see are "standard." There'll be a needle valve for high end adjustment, perhaps another for idle adjustment. A throttle barrel stop screw will adjust the travel of the barrel. These almost never need adjustment, unless the throttle doesn't close far enough to provide a good idle. If there's no idle needle, there will be an idle adjustment of some sort, usually an air bleed screw.

Main Needle Valve

The adjustment you'll spend the most time working on is the high-end needle valve. This meters the amount of fuel flowing through the carburetor at speeds above idle. You can use a procedure for setting this valve that is very similar to the way you would set the needle on a two-stroke engine, but there is one significant difference.

With a two-stroke engine, you can roughly adjust the needle valve by watching the color of the exhaust, or by listening for the highest rpm. Four-stroke engines can't be set that way. For one thing, there will be a certain amount of smoke coming from the exhaust of a typical four-stroke, even after its needle valve is set for peak rpm. Additionally, the peak rpm on the ground will almost certainly be much too lean once the engine gets into the air.

So it's important to use a tachometer to set the needle on your four-stroke. I only use photocell type tachometers, which are pointed at the turning blades to read the rpm. I don't believe that the type of tachometer that has to be held against the spinner or prop hub to get a reading is as safe as the photocell type.

To set your needle valve, start with a setting that is too rich, with the needle turned out at least half a turn farther than what sounds like the peak rpm. Open the throttle wide and let the engine run at full speed. Note the rpm reading. Now slowly turn the needle valve in, no more than a quarter turn at a time, and watch the rpm. It will increase as the

engine runs leaner. When it starts to drop off, the setting is too lean. As soon as you see it drop, back the needle valve out a quarter turn. Be patient, and give the engine a chance to run for a few seconds at each needle setting.

Now that you have the needle set a quarter turn out from where the engine starts to lose rpm, watch the tachometer and see if the engine is running smoothly. Make small adjustments to the needle until you reach a point where the engine maintains rpm. Now start to back the needle valve out toward the rich side. When the rpm drops noticeably, turn the needle in two or three clicks—no more—until the rpm stabilizes. You should now be at a needle setting that is slightly on the rich side, but still gives you a stable high rpm. Your final setting needs to be rich, because engines always lean out in the air.

Now perform the famous "point the nose up" test. Have a friend hold your transmitter, and run the engine up to full throttle. With a firm grip on the airplane (beware of the oily exhaust!), pick the plane up and aim the nose within 20 degrees of the vertical. This simulates the attitude the plane will be in right after takeoff when you're climbing out. The engine has to draw fuel uphill and naturally leans out. Does the engine sag? It's too lean. Put it carefully on the ground and readjust the needle. If the engine holds its rpm through at least 30 seconds (count to 30 slowly) of pointing in the air, you can be confident that it won't quit while you're climbing out after you take off.

Idle Adjustment

You should seldom have to tinker with the idle adjustment of an engine. But if you have broken the engine in properly and set the main needle valve for a reliable high end, you might find that the engine idles too fast. Or you might discover that the engine slows down too much when the throttle is closed and is in danger of stopping. Those are clues that you need to tinker with the idle adjustment.

Your engine will have an idle adjustment of one of two types: either an air bleed, or a needle valve.

Air bleed adjustments are simple. An air bleed

consists of a hole drilled into the carburetor, usually at the back, that lets air in when the carb barrel is at the idle position. There is a screw that can be turned in to close off this hole; the screw is usually mounted on the top of the carb body. Turning this screw in reduces the amount of air coming in, and richens the mixture; turning it out has the opposite effect.

To adjust an air bleed, first sight down the hole and see where it is set. I've made the embarrassing mistake of tinkering with an air bleed screw without realizing that it was backed out so far that the bleed hole was wide open. You don't get much adjustment *that* way!

With the engine running at idle, check the tachometer reading. Most four-stroke engines I've run will idle between 2000 and 3000 rpm. They can sometimes be coaxed lower, but you must be careful to set the idle where the engine will show no tendency to quit.

Adjust the air bleed screw a quarter turn at a time, giving the engine at least 20 seconds between changes to adjust to the new setting. Tune for reliable idle, and feel out how rich the idle can be set. To test the setting, rapidly advance the throttle to full. If the engine bogs down and gasps for a second before hitting smooth rpm at high throttle, the idle is probably set too rich.

Sometimes you may find that the best idle setting that you can achieve still lets the engine sag out when you advance the throttle. If this happens, retune the main needle valve as described above. You may find that the idle adjustment has affected the setting of the main needle.

A carburetor that has an idle needle is adjusted in a very similar way to the air bleed type. The idle needle allows a much finer adjustment of idle speed, and is a little more versatile than an air bleed adjustment. Use your tachometer, and set the needle slightly to the rich side of a reliable idle.

Once you've got an idle setting you like, *always* check and reset the high end needle valve! On many engines, these two controls have a large effect on each other. You will notice this more on engines with two needle valves. Consult the instructions that came with your engine for specifics.

BREAKING-IN FOUR-STROKE ENGINES

Any new engine needs to be broken in to allow the moving parts to wear into a good fit with each other. This is particularly important for the piston and cylinder; see Chapter 7 on two-stroke engines for more discussion of this.

Careful breaking-in is more important with a four-stroke engine than with a two-stroke. This is principally because there are a lot more moving parts in four-stroke engines. Fortunately, it's an easy procedure. And it gives you a very good chance to tinker with the engine, feel out how it performs and what it'll do, and how to adjust it.

First Start

The first thing you should do with a new engine is thoroughly read the instructions. All engines vary, and you can be assured that the engineers who designed the engine know best how to make it perform! Even if you already own one of the engines, check the instructions to see if any changes have been made to the engine. The manufacturers often add to the instructions, based on the advice gained from having production examples of the engine in use.

When I start a four-stroke engine for the first time, I like to be sure I'm working from the rich end of the needle setting. I also like to be sure that I have plenty of fuel in the engine, even if this means starting out flooded. This way, I avoid cranking a dry engine and I learn how well the engine draws fuel. But I always start out hand-flipping an engine, and never use an electric starter at first. Applying an electric starter to a flooded engine can do serious damage! If it becomes necessary to use an electric starter, I always disconnect the fuel line, unscrew the glow plug, put a cloth over the plug hole, and spin the engine with the starter to be certain it isn't flooded.

Once I have the engine mounted in my test stand, the throttle attached to the linkage, and the recommended prop fitted, I turn the needle valve out three full turns. Then, with the throttle wide open, I choke the carburetor, either covering the air inlet with my finger or using a choke valve if the engine has one. Two or three flips, no more, should bring plenty of fuel into the carburetor and the cylinder. I then open the air inlet and pull the prop through carefully, sensing the amount of resistance as it goes through the compression stroke. If the engine is flooded (yes, it's possible to flood it with two or three flips!), it might not move over compression at all. Don't force it! Flip the prop backwards and forwards against the resistance, through the intake and exhaust cycles. The valves will open and breathe more air into the cylinder head, eventually clearing the raw fuel out of the combustion chamber.

Now connect the battery to the plug. Close the throttle to idle, and open it to about one-third. Holding the prop blade firmly (in your fist is best), pull it through compression. You should feel a bump as the fuel mixture ignites. That bump means the engine is ready to start. Glance at your battery connector, fuel lines, and throttle linkage to make sure everything is ready for the engine to start. Then put your chicken stick against the prop blade, turn it until it's against compression, and flip it smartly.

Chances are the engine will light right off. More likely, it'll pop once. Keep flipping until the engine starts, or is clearly dry. Then disconnect the battery and choke the engine again.

If the engine starts, surges to high rpm, and stops abruptly, you're too lean. On the other hand, if it starts and blubbers, it's too rich. It will run at a very rich setting, and that's where you want it at this point.

Once you have the engine running, as rich as it'll continue to run, remove the glow plug connector and slowly advance the throttle to full open. If the engine dies when the connector is removed, it's still too rich. When you have it running rich and wide open, tinker with the needle to make sure you have it just as rich as it will run. Then let it run just like that for 15 minutes.

During this run, you will probably notice some black gook oozing out around the exhaust pipe. That's aluminum powder, caused by the wearing in

of the moving parts. Since the engine is running so rich, there's plenty of unburned oil to move all this powder out of the engine. At the end of this run, let the engine cool down for 15 minutes or so. Then crank it up and run it for another 15 minutes with the needle valve leaned out half a turn.

Now you have half an hour of rich, cool running on your engine. It should be ready for you to find the right needle valve setting. Using your tachometer, go in on the needle until you start to see a loss of rpm. As soon as the rpm sags, back off the needle half a turn. Let the engine run at this setting for another 10 minutes. You can now consider the engine ready to be installed in a plane.

As you fly this new engine, remember that it will be breaking in and improving over the next few flights. Make sure it's running rich when you fly it. After the first five or six flights, you can peak the needle valve as described earlier.

Adjusting Valves

When four-stroke engines first came on the scene, people were continually asking about adjusting the valves. I guess that since poppet valves were only familiar to folks from their car engines, they thought that the same kind of maintenance would be needed. Actually, they were quite right: Poor valve adjustment can cause exactly the same problems in a model four-stroke as in a car engine. But the valves in the model engine have not been a source of trouble in practice.

All model four-stroke engines (except the ones with rotary valves, such as the Webra and HP engines) have valve assemblies that can be easily adjusted. The adjustments are on the rocker arms, above the valve pushrods. On Enya engines and some OS engines, the pushrods are in the back; on Saito engines, they're in front. On all but the Saito .30, the pushrods run in protective tubes and have housings covering the rocker arms. They're not hard to find!

Do They Need Adjusting? Before you adjust the valves on your four-stroke, ask yourself if it really needs it. Have you noticed a marked falloff in rpm? Has the engine been knocking, backfiring, or kicking its prop off? Are you sure it's not doing this because the main needle valve is set too lean?

Ordinarily, the only reason to adjust the valves is wear on the pushrods, which results in less valve opening because the rods are shorter. This will show up on some engines after the first hour of running, and is the last indication that the engine is completely broken in. These pushrods are specially hardened. They may wear slightly at first, but will seldom continue to do so. Check the engine instructions to see when they recommend checking the valves.

Performing the Adjustment. To adjust the valves, remove the valve covers and the glow plug. Turn the engine over until the piston is at top dead center. Both valves will be closed, and there will be a gap between the tops of the pushrods and the bearing surfaces of the rocker arms. This gap is what you adjust.

Many four-stroke engines come with a feeler gauge, a thin strip of metal that is the right thickness to slip into the rocker-pushrod gap when it's correct. O.S. and Saito four-strokes have them; Enyas come with a set of wrenches and a screwdriver. Before you loosen the valve adjusting mechanism, slip the feeler gauge into the gap to make sure that the valve really needs adjusting.

Most rocker arms have an adjustment assembly that consists of a slotted screw held in place by a hex nut. Insert a small screwdriver into the slot, and hold it in position while you loosen the nut with a spanner wrench. Don't use pliers; no matter how

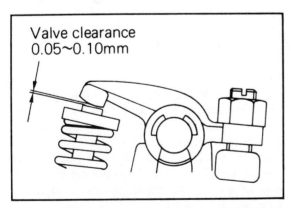

Valve clearance
0.05~0.10mm

Valve clearances rarely need adjustment; you should check them after the engine is broken in. Many engines include a feeler gauge, wrench, and screwdriver to make this easier. (Illustration courtesy Altech Marketing)

careful you are, they always slip.

Once the nut is loosened, slip the feeler gauge into the gap; if it won't go in, turn the screw out until it does. Adjust the screw until the feeler gauge slides smoothly in and out, without binding and without moving vertically. Now, holding the screw where you want it with the screwdriver, tighten the nut. Check the gap again and tinker with the adjustment if necessary. Now do the other one.

You should have to perform this operation rarely. I check the valves once a year on four-stroke engines I use a lot. They seldom need adjustment. If you have one of the very oldest four-strokes, such as the original O.S. 60, you should check the valves a little more often. Modern engines all have hardened pushrods.

FOUR-STROKE MAINTENANCE

Four-stroke engines require the same kind of regular maintenance as two-strokes, only more so. With any model engine, you must be aware of the possibility of internal rust.

Fred Fischer of MRC has worked on model engines from the time the first Enya four-strokes were introduced, and once ran the repair department for MRC. He's seen a lot of engines come in with repairs that could have been prevented. Here's what he says:

"Although Enya engines have suffered from a reputation of bad bearings, it is not due to poor quality or a design flaw. It has been traced to the fuels we use, our cleaning and storage habits, and the basic use of the engine. Some people use too much nitro in the fuel, they underprop the engine so it overrevs in the air, and they allow the burnt fuel to sit in the engine.

"The bottom end of a four-cycle engine is often lubricated by blow-by fuel—burnt fuel that shoots past the piston ring. Burnt fuel contains *nitric and formic acids!* The alcohol in the fuel is hygroscopic; it draws moisture out of the air and promotes rust. This gives the engine a one-two punch if it isn't kept clean on the inside. O.S. and Saito engines have suffered from this syndrome but to a lesser extent because they do not develop as much power and stress as an Enya.

"The rules? Use low (10 percent or less) nitromethane, keep to castor oil-based fuels, drain your engine dry and pump a little kerosene through the oil drain in and out of the engine to neutralize the acids and protect against rust."

Good advice. I generally use 12 percent nitro or less in four-stroke engines. As we'll see, higher nitro doesn't make a four-stroke engine produce more rpm. Using a fuel with less nitromethane means that there's less unburned nitro in the fuel residue to turn into nitric acid.

Running the engine dry is a good policy for any engine after the last flight of the day. The procedure is simple: Before you pump the tank dry after the last flight, fire up the engine again. Making sure you've got a good grip on the plane, open the throttle wide. Now disconnect the fuel line. The engine will run out the last of its fuel and quit, nice and dry on the inside. Remember that alcohol attracts moisture out of the air . . . you don't want to leave any in the engine!

All four-strokes have an oil outlet vent on the crankcase. As Fred says, this is a handy point for injecting some light oil to neutralize the fuel residue and coat the bearings. I keep some Marvel Mystery Oil in a small fuel bulb. Ordinary transmission fluid (not Type F) works well, too. Avoid sewing machine oil or any oil that isn't intended to be used at high temperatures. At the end of a day's flying, I give each engine a shot of Marvel oil in the tube that lets the crankcase oil out of the engine compartment. Then I turn the engine over a few times to distribute the oil throughout the crankcase.

Storing a Four-Stroke

When you store an engine, you should load it with oil as above, then remove the glow plug and put a few drops of oil into the combustion chamber. Turn the engine over a few times. This will work the oil through the intake and exhaust ports. Then seal the engine in a plastic bag to keep moisture out.

Varnishing

The combustion products left in an engine can cause corrosion, and that's the most important thing to guard against. But you'll sometimes encounter another fuel-related problem. It's caused by the fact that castor oil can form a hard, paint-like coating when it's heated. This is commonly called *varnish*, and it can foul the valve seats and coat the cylinder liner, sticking the piston in place.

The only way to avoid varnish buildup is to keep your engine clean. Follow the procedures outlined above to make sure no fuel is left in the engine. After each flight, before shutting down the engine, pinch off or remove the fuel line so it runs itself dry.

Varnishing is a problem, but it's not the sort of thing that will trouble you if you follow proper procedure. Don't be tempted to use a fuel with no castor oil in the lubricant mix; this can give you overheating problems. On the other hand, selecting the right fuel can help prevent varnishing. At least one fuel maker I know of, Red Max, includes anti-varnishing agents in their four-stroke fuel.

The usual place that people encounter varnish is on the outside of the engine. Unburned fuel on the cylinder head or the outside of the exhaust pipe will cook into brown goo after a few months of running. Standale Aircraft Products sells an excellent cleaner that dissolves this stuff; you just brush it on and wipe it off. Don't be tempted to scrub it off; you'll scar the aluminum.

FUELS

There are several different brands of four-stroke fuel on the market. Which one to use is largely a matter of personal preference and experience. I'll tell you about some of my experience with different brands. This doesn't cover all that's available, of course.

Before we get specific, here are two cautions to keep in mind: First of all, be sure to use a fuel with at least *some* castor oil in the lubricant mix. Castor oil has superior heat transfer properties and will help protect the engine from overheating. Second, and most important, remember that you get what you pay for. The cheapest fuel you can get is seldom the best for your engine, either in terms of performance or longevity.

When you want more power or speed from a two-stroke engine, you generally use a fuel with a higher percentage of nitromethane. Not so with four-strokes. Higher nitro content will not increase the top end rpm of the engine; after all, most four-strokes are limited by design to a max rpm anyway. Nitro in four-stroke fuel will improve the reliability of the engine's idle and allow you to set the idle to lower rpm. This is why you don't find four-stroke fuels with a wide range of nitro content; standard is 10 to 12 percent.

I have had very good success with Red Max four-stroke fuel. It's sold in 10 and 15 percent nitro strengths. I generally use the 10 percent mix in sport models with the engine mounted upright, and 15 percent in models with inverted or side-mounted engines. The hotter fuel helps keep the cylinder firing at low rpm and rich idle settings.

I've also had very good success with Cool Power four-stroke fuel. JMD Fuel Labs was one of the first out with a four-stroke fuel, and their 12 percent mix is one of my favorites for all-around use. SIG Manufacturing is now mixing a range of four-stroke fuels. And I've tried a gallon of Avgas four-stroke fuel from Ace RC with excellent results.

Which one should you pick? Try a few and decide for yourself. Stick with 10 to 12 percent nitro unless your engine is mounted inverted or has given you some trouble on idle. Watch the magazines (especially the engine columns, such as Clarence Lee's excellent series in *RCM*) for news about new fuels. Ask your friends what they've found; a little experience is the best guide you can have.

SOME POPULAR FOUR-STROKE ENGINES

I've owned and run samples of just about every four-stroke engine available in the USA, and learned a lot in the process. Each brand of engine has certain characteristics that seem to be common no matter what size the engine is. I'll describe some of my experiences; you may have different things happen when you try them out, but I think you'll find this overview helpful just the same.

Enya. The first four-stroke I ever owned was an Enya .35, and I still have a lot of affection for the engine. I've never met an Enya four-stroke I didn't like. They are consistently more powerful for their size than comparable four-strokes. They can be a little cranky because of this; one of their major quirks

is a tendency to backfire and kick the prop loose if they're leaned out too far. This can be prevented by running the engine where you should have it in the first place—slightly rich.

Many Enya four-strokes come with an extra gasket for the cylinder head. If you consistently have problems with the prop kicking loose, you can insert this gasket between the cylinder and head. You will need to regap the valves after doing this. Adding this gasket will reduce the engine's compression, which will reduce power slightly, but will cure the tendency to kick the prop. After running the engine for a while, consider removing the gasket and trying again; as the engine breaks in, its running characteristics will improve.

The Enya .46 is worthy of note. It's designed to fit into most kits that call for a .40 two-stroke engine. Properly propped (11-7 is the best size I've found for the .46), it will produce ¾ horsepower, which is more than most common sport .40 two-strokes. It's a scale builder's delight.

The Enya .80 is a direct descendant of the .60, with the cylinder bored out and a slightly longer stroke. It's actually a few ounces lighter than the .60 and considerably more powerful.

There are two 1.20 size Enya four-strokes. The "straight" 1.20 is an excellent workhorse engine based on the design of the smaller Enyas. The R120 is a special engine, designed for international-class aerobatics competition. It has a custom carb that allows precise adjustment of the fuel mix, especially at idle. It's quite a bit more expensive than the "straight" 1.20, so I recommend that you consider the cheaper engine for sport flying.

Most of the Enya four-strokes have their glow plugs positioned on the front of the cylinder. Don't be tempted to use a cylindrical glow plug connector on them. When you pull it off, you can rap your knuckles on the back of the spinning prop. I only had to do this once . . . don't *you* do it at all! Use a remote connector permanently wired to the plug. Remote connectors are made by Model Products and McDaniel RC; most hobby shops have them.

At this writing, Enya has announced a very exciting new engine, a V-twin. I've only looked at specs and drawings so far, but it should be a power-

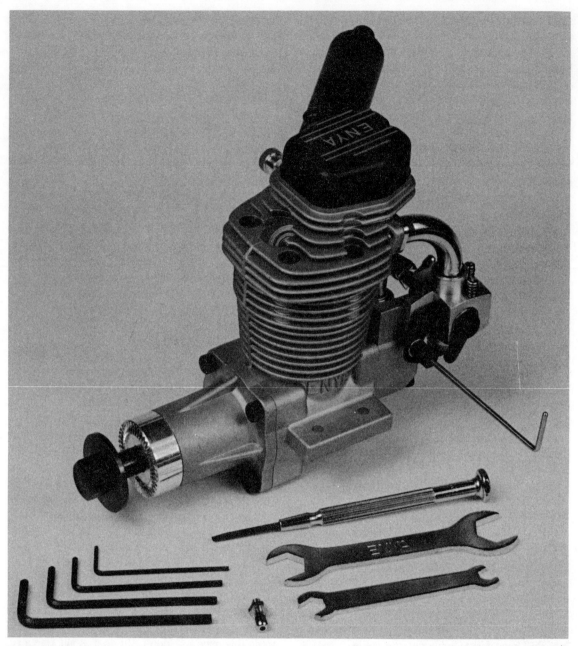

The Enya .90 and 1.20 four-strokes are based on the same crankcase. All Enya four-strokes come with a set of tools and a pressure tap for the muffler. (Photo courtesy Altech Marketing)

house. It has a single carburetor, so tuning will be simplified. The V-twin arrangement should help eliminate problems associated with inverted mounting. This engine could be a quarter scale builder's dream.

Saito. I am very fond of Saito four-strokes. Saito makes only two types of engines—four-stroke and steam! They've been at it for a long time and have an excellent reputation; in my experience, that

The new Enya VT240 four-stroke is the only V-twin four-stroke in mass production. Each cylinder has its own carburetor. It can produce 3.2 horsepower, turning an 18-8 prop at 11,000 rpm. (Photo courtesy Altech Marketing)

reputation is well-deserved. They are also quite inexpensive in comparison with other four-strokes.

Saito engines aren't as powerful as Enyas, and are slightly heavier. They make up for this by being the easiest-handling engines I've ever played with. They tolerate a wide range of props, and can be lugged down with a large prop for a slow-flying scale ship.

The earlier Saito designs have glow plugs that are positioned in such a way that you can't get a standard connector (like a Ni-Starter or Nilite) off them without hitting the prop. The little Saito .30 is like this. Use a remote glow plug connector like a HeadLock Remote for these engines.

Saito four-strokes seem to tolerate a wide range of glow plugs as well. I've used K&B Short plugs with excellent results. As mentioned elsewhere, the use of a special four-stroke plug (Fox, O.S., or Sonic-Tronics) will improve the idle. Fuel isn't a problem either; my Saitos run happily on any 10 percent sport fuel. I do make certain that the fuel has castor oil in the lubricant mix, to reduce the chance of overheating.

Saito makes several multi-cylinder four-strokes. I've owned their little .90 twin for several years, and have been very happy with it. Saito also makes a big 270 twin that has become very popular for Giant models; it makes an excellent replacement for a Quadra-size engine if you'd rather work with a glow engine than a gas engine. The latest offering from Saito is a magnificent five-cylinder radial engine.

O.S. The first production four-strokes came from O.S. Engines. That original engine, the .60, has been replaced by a more powerful .61, but is still flown in a lot of places. In general, these engines maintain the excellent reputation that O.S. has earned with its two-stroke engines.

O.S. four-strokes really must be run with a special four-stroke glow plug. It improves the idle dramatically; there's just no reason to struggle with a standard plug. The ones I've run seem to prefer 10 percent four-stroke fuel after breaking in for about 30 minutes on 10 percent two-stroke fuel.

The O.S. .20 four-stroke is worthy of note. It's the smallest commercially available four-stroke, and it's a gem. If you have a small scale or sport model

Saito makes a wide range of four-stroke engines, noted for their smooth running. Shown here, left to right, are the Saito .30, .45, 1.20, and .90 flat twin. All come with a set of tools. (Photo courtesy United Model Products)

The O.S. Gemini Twin comes in two sizes: 1.60 and 2.40 cu. in. displacement. The single carburetor makes it easy to adjust. These have become very popular among scale model builders. (Photo courtesy Great Planes Distributing)

Webra makes a series of unique four-stroke engines that have a rotary drum valve in the cylinder head. The drum is turned by a toothed belt driven by the crankshaft. Shown here are the Webra .40 (left) and .90 four-strokes. A .60 and .80 are also available. (Photo by Jennifer Pratt)

that's designed for an .09 to .15 two-stroke engine, the .20 will fly it well. It doesn't seem to object to running inverted, although the needle setting is more difficult to find. If you mount the engine inverted, make sure the centerline of the fuel tank is level with the carburetor.

The O.S. Gemini Twin blazed the trail for multi-cylinder four-strokes. It fits beautifully in a Quarter Scale Cub or Aeronca Champ, or just about any twin-powered classic lightplane. Two sizes of the Gemini are available.

O.S. has released two spectacular four-strokes: the Pegasus inline four-cylinder, and the Sirius five-cylinder radial. I haven't run either of these engines, but I've spoken to several people who have and they're very pleased with them. The Pegasus would be a good substitute for a Quadra or similar size gasoline engine. Both of these engines are priced in the $1500 range, so you won't see hundreds of them around.

Webra. Webra came out with a very interesting line of four-stroke engines several years ago. Instead of poppet valves, there's a drum in the head of the engine. The drum rotates on its vertical axis, and is driven from the crankshaft by a toothed belt on the front of the engine. The intake, glow plug, and exhaust are mounted around the top of the cylinder head. As the drum turns, a hole in it that leads to the cylinder passes the carburetor, allowing fuel

into the chamber. Then the hole moves to the glow plug, which ignites the fuel. Finally, the hole travels to the exhaust outlet.

There are several advantages to this unique setup. For one thing, there's no danger of "floating" the valves at high speed. Floating occurs with a poppet-valve engine when the springs that return the valves to their seats can't work fast enough and the valves aren't quite closed when combustion starts. This means that these engines have a wider range of useful rpm than some four-strokes. You can also use smaller props at higher rpm. The drum valve will help to prevent pre-ignition, since the glow plug is only exposed to the combustion chamber when the piston is near top dead center.

Webra makes three engines in this design: a .40, a .60, and an .80. I've run the .40 quite a bit, and have been quite satisfied with it. It's currently flying a small scale model with a 9-7 prop.

HP. The German manufacturer HP has produced two four-strokes that use rotary valves. I'm told that they're no longer in production, but there are plenty of them around. Two sizes were made, a .21 and a .49.

The HP four-strokes use a rotating valve shaped like a cone, with the point downward. It is turned by a shaft running in a sleeve up the back of the engine. As the cone rotates, it exposes the inlet, glow plug, and exhaust to the combustion chamber. As with other rotary valve four-strokes, there's no danger in overspinning these engines.

In order to lubricate the shaft, the HP four-strokes have a curious exhaust arrangement. There's a tap on the exhaust pipe where you'd expect to find one for tank pressurization. Instead, you use a short length of fuel line to connect it to another nipple at the top of the vertical shaft housing. This ducts some of the exhaust down through the shaft housing, through the crankcase pan, and out another nipple near the front bearing. Unburned oil in the exhaust lubricates the gears at the ends of the shaft. You can connect your tank pressure line to the forward nipple.

I've run the HP .21 quite a bit. I found that the exotic exhaust setup is unnecessary, since the crankcase seems to get plenty of lubrication from fuel that blows by the piston. Pressurizing the fuel tank from the forward nipple also seems to provide too much pressure; I had a lot of trouble getting a needle setting with the recommended setup. Finally, I read a suggestion in Clarence Lee's engine column in *RC Modeler* magazine. Clarence said to try pressurizing the tank directly from the nipple on the exhaust pipe, just as you would with any other engine. I tried it and my needle setting problems went away. Just in case, I squirt a little oil in the nipple at the

top of the vertical shaft at the end of each day's flying. I've had no problems with the engine since trying this fix.

Technopower. Some years ago, an engineer in Ireland designed a miniature radial four-stroke engine. It gained quite a reputation, but not much commercial success. The design was sold to an American company called Technopower II, and has since found the success it deserves. Now there are Technopower radials available in three, five, seven and nine-cylinder configurations. The five and seven-cylinder motors are available either as glow engines or set up for ignition use with miniature spark plugs.

Technopower engines are largely handmade, and are real works of art. The prices range from $700 to $1800. I've had the chance to run a five-cylinder Technopower, and was very impressed with the easy handling. The carburetor is a standard one, adjusted exactly the same way you adjust other four-strokes. I didn't notice any bad habits at all.

One thing to be aware of when running a Technopower engine (or any radial) is that oil will collect in the lower cylinders. If there's a lot of oil, it could cause a hydraulic lock when the engine is turned over the first time. You should remove the glow plugs from the lower cylinders and turn the engine through several times before starting it.

THE FUTURE

You can look for more innovations in four-stroke design in the future. Four-strokes are continually being upgraded to deliver more power. Mark II versions of Enya, O.S., and Saito engines are all being delivered.

You're also likely to see some entirely new four-stroke engines. K&B has been working with a prototype 1.20 four-stroke designed by master engine man Bill Wisniewski. It incorporates four overhead valves. I don't know when this engine will be available, since K&B is busy filling orders for their excellent new .20 and .45 two-strokes, but they're serious about it.

I've also heard rumors that Fox is developing a four-stroke. Given Fox's excellent reputation, they won't release it until they're satisfied with it.

H.P. produced two four-strokes that used rotary drum valves. The valves were driven by a shaft running up the back of the engine. Oil was taken from the exhaust and ducted down the back, through the crankcase pan, and out the front. This is the H.P. 21; they also made a .49. (Photo by Jennifer Pratt)

Technopower makes a series of remarkable radial four-strokes. This is their seven-cylinder radial; it has a single carburetor at the back, feeding the cylinders through intake pipes. Like full-size engines, the cylinders fire in order. (Photo courtesy Technopower II, Inc.)

Appendix A

Radio Control Manufacturers and Suppliers

Ace R C
116 West 19th St
Higginsville, MO 64037
Electronic kits, model kits, famous Silver Seven radios, Four Stroke Squadron.

Airtronics, Inc.
11 Autry
Irvine, CA 92718-2709
RC systems, kits.

Astro Flight
13311 Beach Ave.
Venice, CA 90291
Electric flight systems, kits.

B & B Specialties
14234 Cleveland Road
Granger, IN 46530
Quadra engines, Giant model supplies.

Balsa USA Incorporated
201 Third Avenue
Menominee, MI 49858
Kits, including Giant Scale.

Bee Hive Model Aircraft
Box 744
Layton, UT 84041
Old Timer kits.

Beemer RC West Distributors, Inc.
7725 E Redfield Dr Suite 105
Scottsdale, AZ 85260
Multiplex RC systems, sales and service.

Bell Rock Industries
6486 Hwy 179
Sedona, AZ 86336
Accessories, sanding tools.

Bob Martin RC Models
1520 Acoma Lane #C
Lake Havasu City, AZ 86403-2051
Sailplane kits.

Bob Violett Models
1373 Citrus Road
Winter Springs, FL 32708
Ducted fan kits, fan units, building supplies, composite construction materials.

Bridi Aircraft Designs, Inc.
23625 Pineforest Lane
Harbor City, CA 90710
Airplane kits, glow plugs, accessories.

Byron Originals
Box 279 Highway 59 and 175
Ida Grove, IA 51445
Giant Scale and ducted fan kits, engines, accessories.

C. B. Associates Incorporated
21658 Cloud Way
Hayward, CA 94545
Accessories, Giant Scale supplies.

Cannon RC Systems
Lightweight miniature RC systems.

Carl Goldberg Models
4732 W. Chicago Ave.
Chicago, IL 60651
Trainer planes, scale kits, Jet adhesives, accessories.

Carlson Engine Imports
814 E. Marconi Ave.
Phoenix, AZ 85022
Imported engines: PAW, Aurora, Mills and Taplin reproductions, rare engines.

Champion Model Aero. Co.
P.O. Box 891
Woodbridge, NJ 07095
Airplane kits, including Old Timers.

Chevron
P.O. Box 2480
Sandusky, OH 44870
Perfect brand paint.

Circus Hobbies
3132 South Highland Drive
Las Vegas, NV 89109
JR radio systems, kits, engines, accessories.

Cleveland Model and Supply
10309 Detroit Ave.
Cleveland, OH 44102
Hundreds of plans for scale and Old Timer models, famous Cleveland Kits.

CompuServe
5000 Arlington Centre Blvd.
Columbus, OH 43220
Personal computer network, includes ModelNet.

Condor Trading Company
27482 Capricho
Mission Viejo, CA 92692
Picco engines, electric motors, accessories.

Coverite
420 Babylon Road
Horsham, PA 19044
Covering materials, kits, accessories.

Cox Hobbies
1525 E. Warner
Santa Ana, CA 92705
.049 engines, kits, RC systems, ready-to-fly planes.

Craft Air Incorporated
20115 Nordhoff Street
Chatsworth, CA 91311
Kits, accessories.

Dave Brown Products
4560 Layhigh Road
Hamilton, OH 45013
Accessories, wheels, RC Flight Simulator for personal computers.

Dave Platt Models, Inc.
6940 Northwest 45th St.
Plantation, FL 33313
Scale model kits.

Davey Systems Corp.
1 Wood Lane
Malvern, PA 19355
Sailplane kits, electric power kits, winches, electric motors, accessories.

Davis Diesel Development
Box 141
Milford, CT 06460
Conversion kits to Dieselize glow engines, accessories, fuel, tools.

Du-Bro Products
480 Bonner Road
Wauconda, IL 60084
Accessories, tools, wheels, hardware.

Dura Craft
1007 Orchard Grove Dr.
Royal Oak, MI 48067
Dura Plane trainer kits.

Dynathrust
2541 N E 11th Court
Pompano Beach, FL 33062
Propellers for large engines.

Edson Enterprises
17 Speer Place
Nutley, NJ 07110
Accessories, adjustable engine mounts.

Eldon J. Lind Company
Los Alamitos, CA 90720
Accessories, building boards, tools.

Eric Clutton—P.A.W. Diesels USA
913 Cedar Lane
Tullahoma, TN 37388-3167
Imported Diesel engines, fuel.

F H S Supply
Rt 5 Box 68
Clover, SC 29710
Red Max fuels, Diesel fuel, custom blends.

Flyline Models
10643 Ashby Place
Fairfax, VA 22030
Schoolyard Scale kits.

Fox Manufacturing
5305 Towson Ave.
Fort Smith, AR 72901
Model engines, spinners, glow plugs, tools, accessories.

Futaba
555 West Victoria
Compton, CA 90220
RC systems, accessories.

Gorham Model Products
23961 Craftsman Road
Calabasas, CA 91302
Helicopter kits, accessories, gyros.

Great Planes Manufacturing
706 West Bradley
Urbana, IL 61801
Model kits, accessories.

Grish Brothers
P.O. Box 248
St. John, IN 46373
Propellers, accessories.

H & N Electroncis
10937 Rome Beauty Drive
California City, CA 93505
Electronic accessories, Supersafe solder flux.

Harry B. Higley & Sons, Incorporated
433 Arquilla Drive
Glenwood, IL 60425
Accessories, tools.

Hayes Products
1558 Osage Street
San Marcos, CA 92069
Tanks, motor mounts, accessories.

Herb's Model Motors
Box 61
Forksville, PA 18616
Antique reproduction engines and parts.

High Point Products
3013 Mary Kay Lane
Glenview, IL 60025
Prop balancing tools.

Hobby Horn
15173 Moran Street
Westminster, CA 92683
Old Timer kits, electric kits, and flight systems.

Hobby Lobby International
Route 3 Franklin Pike Cir.
Brentwood, TN 37027
Graupner kits, accessories, tools, large catalog.

Hobby Shack
18480 Bandilier Circle
Fountain Valley, CA 92708
Kits, ready-to-fly planes, RC systems, engines, accessories, large catalog.

Indy RC
10620 N. College Ave.
Indianapolis, IN 46280
Kits, engines, ready-to-fly planes, large catalog.

J & Z Products
25029 South Vermont Avenue
Harbor City, CA 90710
Props, spinners, accessories.

J M D Fuel Labs
P.O. Box 235
North Olmstead, OH 44070
Custom blended fuels.

J' Tec
164 School St.
Daly City, CA 94014
Engine mounts, hardware, in-cowl mufflers, accessories.

Jet Hangar Hobbies
12554 Centralia Road Lakewood, CA 90715
Ducted fan kits, fan power systems.

John Pond Old Time Plan Service
Box 3215
San Jose, CA 95156
Old Timer plans.

Jomar
2028 Knightsbridge
Cincinnati, OH 45244
Electric motor speed controllers, engine sync systems, accessories.

K & B Manufacturing
12152 South Woodruff Avenue
Downey, CA 90241
Engines, fuels, epoxy paints, accessories.

Kraft Midwest
117 E. Main St.
Northville, MI 48167
RC system repair and tuning, Kraft radio parts.

Kress Technology
27 Mill Road
Lloyd Harbor, NY 11743
Tanks, accessories, ducted fan power systems.

Kustom Kraftsmanship
P.O. Box 2699
Laguna Hills, CA 92653
Accessories for .049 engines.

Lanier RC
Oakwood Road
Oakwood, GA 30566
Ready-to-fly airplane kits, accessories.

Larry Jolly Models
5501 West Como
Santa Ana, CA 92703
Sailplane and electric flight model kits.

Leisure Electronics
22971 B Triton Way
Laguna Hills, CA 92653
Electric flight systems, chargers, Old Timer kits.

MRC
2500 Woodbridge
Edison, NJ 08817
Ready-to-fly airplanes, RC systems, radios, engines, model rockets, RC cars.

Mac's Products
8020 18th Avenue
Sacramento, CA 95826
Mufflers and tuned pipes for most model engines, accessories.

Major Decals
21 Fisher Ave.
E. Longmeadow, MA 01028
Decal and stick-on insignia sets and designs.

Mark's Models
1578 Osage
San Marcos, CA 92065
Fun scale kits, sailplane kits, accessories.

Mc Daniel RC Service
12421 Ransom Dr.
Glendale, MD 20769
Accessories, Ni-Starter glow plug batteries.

Micro Model Engineering
1301 West Lafayette
Sturgis, MI 49091
Reproduction parts for ignition engines.

Micro- X
P.O. Box 1063
Lorain, OH 44055
Kits, supplies, accessories.

Midwest Products
400 South Indiana
Hobart, IN 46342
Kits, accessories, wood and building supplies.

Miniature Aircraft Supply
2594 N. Orange Blossom Trail
Orlando, FL 32804
Helicopter kits, parts, and accessories.

Model Aviation Products
368 Tuckerton Road
Medford, NJ 08055
Mufflers, tuned pipes, accessories.

Model Engineering of Norwalk
54 Chestnut Hill
Norwalk, CT 06851
Kits, chargers, accessories.

Model Magic Products
P.O. Box 7784
St. Paul, MN 55119
Model Magic Filler, adhesives, fuel tubing, accessories.

Model Products Corp.
P.O. Box 314
Pompton Plains, NJ 07444
Head Lock glow plug connectors, D-Hinges, accessories.

Moody Tools
42-60 Crompton Ave.
East Greenwich, RI 02818
Precision miniature tool sets.

Morgan's Hobby Enterprises
200 West Lee St.
Enterprise, AL 36330
Cool Power fuel.

Nick Ziroli Models
29 Edgar Dr.
Smithtown, NY 11787
Giant Scale plans, accessories.

Norm Rosenstock Plans
94 Cedar Dr.
Plainview, NY 11803
Giant Scale plans.

Novak Electronics
2709 Orange Avenue, C
Santa Ana, CA 92707
RC receivers, speed controllers, electronic accessories.

Off the Ground Models, Inc.
606 C West Anthony Drive
Urbana, IL 61801
Sailplane kits.

Ohio Superstar Model Products
11376 Ridgeway Road
Kensington, OH 44427
Kits, accessories.

PIC Penn International Chemicals
943 Stierlin Road
Mountain View, CA 94043
Adhesives, chemical products.

PK Products
P.O. Box 6226
Hayward, CA 94540
Giant scale motors, accessories.

Pacer Technology
1600 Dell Ave
Campbell, CA 95008
Adhesives.

Paul K. Guillow, Inc.
40 New Salem St.
Wakefield, MA 01880
Scale model kits.

Peck-Polymers
9962 Prospect Suite L
Santee, CA 92071
Kits, supplies, RC blimp kit, CO_2 motors.

Pettit Paint Co. Inc.
36 Pine St.
Rockaway Boro, NJ 07866
HobbyPoxy adhesives and paints.

Pica Products
2657 N E 188th St.
Miami, FL 33180
Kits, adhesives, accessories.

Polk's Hobbies
346 Bergen Ave.
Jersey City, NJ 07304
Kits, engines, RC systems, accessories, tools.

Progress Manufacturing Company
P.O. Box 1306
Manhattan, KS 66502
Propellers.

RAM
4734 N. Milwaukee Ave.
Chicago, IL 60630
Electric accessories, speed controllers, boat kits.

RJL Industries
P.O. Box 5654
Pasadena, CA 91107
Engines, accessories, parts.

Repla-Tech International, Incorporated
48500 Mc Kenzie Highway
Vida, OR 97488
Photos, plans, and documentation for scale aircraft.

Rhom Products Mfg. Corp.
908 65th St.
Brooklyn, NY 11219
Retractable landing gear, accessories.

Robart
310 North 5th
St. Charles, IL 60714
Tools, accessories.

Robbe Model Sport
180 Township Line Road
Bellemead, NJ 08502
Kits, almost-ready-to-fly airplanes, chargers, accessories.

Rocket City RC Specialties
103 Wholesale Ave N E
Huntsville, AL 35811
Accessories, tools, hinges.

Roush Manufacturing
1728 Bywood St. S E
Canton, OH 44707-1224
Giant scale kits.

Royal Products Corporation
790 West Tennessee Ave.
Denver, CO 80223
Kits, ready-to-fly models, engines, accessories.

SR Batteries
P.O. Box 287
Bellport, NY 11713
High-performance batteries for RC systems, electric flight.

Satellite City
P.O. Box 836
Simi, CA 93062-0836
Hot Stuff CyA adhesives, accessories.

Scale Model Research
418 East Oceanfront
Newport Beach, CA 92661
Scale photos and documentation.

Scande Research, Incorporated
P.O. Box 133
Villa Park, IL 60181
Kits, accessories.

Shamrock Competition Imports
Box 26247
New Orleans, LA 70186
OPS engines, parts, accessories, glow plugs.

SIG Manufacturing
401 S. Front St.
Montezuma, IA 50171
Kits, engines, RC systems, paint and covering, accessories, large catalog.

Sonic-Tronics
7862 Mill Road
Elkins Park, PA 19117
Accessories, glow plugs, fuel pumps.

Standale Aircraft
2648 East Thornwood
Wyoming, MI 49509
Accessories.

Sterling Hobbies Inc.
3620 G St.
Philadelphia, PA 19134
Kits, RC and control line.

Sterner Engineering
661 Moorestown Drive
Bath, PA 18014
Ducted fan accessories and supplies.

Sullivan Products
1 N. Haven St.
Baltimore, MD 21224
Accessories, starters, pushrods, tanks, hardware.

Super Cyclone Engines
P.O. Box 10658
Phoenix, AZ 85064
Reproduction Old Timer engines.

T & D Research Associates
6371 El Cajon Blvd.
San Diego, CA 92115
Edco Sky Devil replica engines, parts.

Tatone Products Corporation
1209 Geneva Avenue
San Francisco, CA 92112
Engine mounts, mufflers, accessories, test stands.

Technopower
610 North Street
Chagrin Falls, OH 44022
Radial four-stroke engines.

Top Flite Models
MonoKote covering, scale and sailplane kits, trainers, props.

Tower Hobbies
1608 Interstate Dr.
Champaign, IL 61821
Kits, engines, radio systems, large catalog.

U. S. Quadra
1032 East Manitowoc Avenue
Oakcreek, WI 53154
Quadra engines, props, accessories for Giant Scale.

Ultra Systems By Da Ca
6303 South 168th St.
Omaha, NE 68144
Field boxes, model support stands, accessories.

United Model Distributors
301 Holbrook Dr.
Wheeling, IL 60090
Engines, ready-to-fly planes.

W. E. Technical Services
P.O. Box 76884
Atlanta, GA 30328
Plans and drawings.

Williams Brothers Inc.
181 Pawnee St.
San Marcos, CA 92069
Parts and accessories for scale models, plastic kits, pilot figures.

Wilshire Model Center
2836 Santa Monica Boulevard
Santa Monica, CA 90404
Electric power systems, props, hard-to-find electric stuff.

Windsor Propeller Company
384 Tesconi Court
Santa Rosa, CA 95401
Master Airscrew props and accessories.

Wing Manufacturing
P.O. Box 33
Crystal Lake, IL 60014
Accessories, foam wing kits, model kits.

World Engines
8960 Rossash Ave.
Cincinnati, OH 45236
Engines, radio systems, ready-to-fly kits, accessories.

Yale Hobby Mfg.
20 Holly Lane
Wallingford, CT 06492
Helicopter blades, parts, and accessories.

Zenith Aviation Books
P.O. Box 1
Osceola, WI 54020
Reference books, magazines, videotapes, and calendars.

Zimpro Marketing
P.O. Box 3076
Oak Ridge, TN 37830
Ready-to-fly kits from Zimbabwe Model Products.

Appendix B

Magazines, Publishers, and Booksellers

Flying Models Magazine
Box 700
Newton, NJ 07860

Hannan's Runway
Box A
Escondido, CA 92025

Historic Aviation
3850 Coronation Road
Eagan, MN 55122

Kalmbach Publishing
1027 N. Seventh St.
Milwaukee, WI 53233

Midwest Technical Publications
1741 Big Bend
St. Louis, MO 63117

Model Airplane News
632 Danbury Road
Georgetown, CT 06829

Model Aviation Magazine
1810 Samuel Morse Drive
Reston, VA 22090

Model Builder Magazine
898 W. 16th St.
Newport Beach, CA 92663-2802

Model Shopper Magazine
524 Second St.
San Francisco, CA 94107

Motorbooks International
729 Prospect Ave.
Osceola, WI 54020

RC Report
P.O. Box 1706
Huntsville, AL 35807

RC Soaring Digest
P.O. Box 269
Peterborough, NH 03458

RC Video Magazine
Box 98
Lafayette, CO 80026

Radio Control Modeler Magazine
120 W. Sierra Madre Blvd.
Sierra Madre, CA 91023

Scale RC Modeler
7950 Deering Ave.
Canoga Park, CA 91304

Squadron/Signal Publications
1115 Crowley Drive
Carrollton, TX 75006

TAB BOOKS Inc.
Blue Ridge Summit, PA 17294

Appendix C

AMA Recognized
Special Interest Groups

Officers' Name and Address	Sec/Treas.	Publication

Electric Aeromodeling Association

Robert A. Sliff, President
P.O. Box 9
Midway City, CA 92655

International Miniature Aircraft Association (IMAA)

		High Flight
Dick Phillips	Bill Wilbur	Les Hard
2070 Wesbrook Drive	P.O. Box 501	2909 W. Mich. Ave
Sidney, BC Canada V8L 4K1	Kittery, ME 03904	Lansing, MI 48917

International Miniature Aerobatic Club (IMAC)

John Lockwood, President	C. Glenn Carter	*IMAC Newsletter*
1696 Griffith Avenue	2020 Gill Port Lane	C. Glenn Carter
Clovis, CA 93612	Walnut Creek, CA 94598	

Miniature Aircraft Combat Association (MACA)

Phil Cartier, President
760 Waltonville RD
Hummestown, PA 17036
(312) 532-7349

Chris Gay
2018 Wessel Ct
St. Charles, IL 60174
(312) 584-6015

MACA Newsletter
Dr. T. R. Passen
P.O. Box 111
Jasonvle, IN 47438

National Association of Scale Aeromodelers (NASA)

John Guenther, President
RR 3, Box 261
Borden, IN 47106

Replica
Burt Dugan
11090 Phyllis Dr
Clio, MI 48420

Navy Carrier Society (NCS)

Pete Mazur, President
5 W. Windsor Court
Aurora, IL 60504

Hi Low Landings
Melvin Schuette
P.O. Box 293
Auburn, KS 66402

National Free Flight Society (NFFS)

Tony Italiano, President
1655 Revere Drive
Brookfield, WI 53005

Free Flight Digest
Robert Meuser
707 Second St
Davis, CA 95616

National Miniature Pylon Racing Association (NMPRA)

Henry Bartle, President
1353 N. Santiago
Santa Ana, CA 92701

Jill Bussell
4803 Fallon Place
Dallas, TX 75227

NMPRA
Karen Yeager
38238 Castle
Romulus, MI 48174

National Society of Radio Controlled Aerobatics (NSRCA)

Craig Millet, President
c/o Gibson, Dunn & Crutcher
P.O. Box 2490
Newport Beach, CA 92660

Suzi Stream
3723 Snowden Avenue
Long Beach, CA 90808

K FACTOR
Betty Stream
3723 Snowden Avenue
Long Beach, CA 90808

National Soaring Society (NSS)

Peter Carr, President
229 Little Avenue
Ridgway, PA 15853

Dick Crowley
16413 E. Stanford Pl.
Aurora, CO 80015

Sailplane
Doug Dorton
3058 Bernina Drive
SLC UT 84118

North American Speed Society

William Wisniewski
9222 Cedar Street
Bellflower, CA 90706

Bev Wisniewski
9222 Cedar Street
Bellflower, CA 90706

Speed Times
Box 82294
North Burnaby, BC

Precision Aerobatics Model Pilots Association (PAMPA)

George Higgins
P.O. Box 561
N. Pembroke, MA 02358

Doug Figgs
329 Lincoln Place
Brooklyn, NY 11238

Pro Stunt News
Windy Urtnowski
9 Union Avenue
Littleferry, NJ 07643

Society of Antique Modelers (SAM)

Sal Taibi, President
4339 Conquista Ave.
Lakewood, CA 90713

Robert Dodds
2005 West Pine
Lodi, CA 95240

Sam Speaks
Jim Adams, Editor
2538 N. Spurgeon St.
Santa Ana, CA 92706

United Scale and Pattern Judges Association

Frank Broach, Sr.
463 S. Harrison Avenue
St. Louis, MO 63122

Russell Knetzger
2625 E. Shorewood Blvd.
Milwaukee, WI 53211

Appendix D

Academy of Model Aeronautics
Insurance Facts

Accident/Medical Coverage

(Applies to individual members only)
This coverage works together with liability protection, but Accident/Medical applies to injury only, to reimburse an AMA member for medical expenses (also to reimburse the beneficiary for loss of life). Property damage is not involved. The Accident/Medical coverage applies to injuries resulting from model operation accidents regardless of who causes the accidents. AMA Liability Protection, however, applies to injury or property damage caused by an AMA member to someone else (see Comprehensive General Liability Coverage). The Accident/Medical coverage works as follows:

1. Provides up to $7,500 each for personal injury, and $1,500 for dismemberment or death.
2. Operates directly—does not require claim action by another person.
3. Pays upon submission of bills or other documents certifying cost of treatment.

4. Applies to model operation, in accordance with the AMA Safety Code.
5. Reimburses only for those expenses not covered by any other health plan.

What to do: If you are injured while engaged in the operation of models, please call the AMA to obtain a medical claim form and detailed instructions for filing your claim.

Fire, Vandalism, and Theft Coverage

(Applies to individual members only)

1. Provides up to $1,000 for loss of models and accessories, including RC equipment. Theft loss claims must be accompanied by a police report and are evaluated in light of the information contained therein; i.e. whether stolen articles were, at the time of theft, in a locked or secured structure or conveyance and whether police found signs of forcible entry.
2. Except for first $100, which is deductible.

3. Coverage is "excess" to any other coverage which may be applicable.

Comprehensive General Liability Coverage

(Applies to individual members, clubs, chapters, and additional insureds)

1. For accidents arising from the operation of model aircraft, rockets, cars, and boats, in accordance with the AMA (or NAR) Safety Code.
2. Up to $1,000,000 per accident for bodily injury and/or property damage, subject to a $1,000,000 annual aggregate limit of liability which applies individually and collectively to all AMA members and additional insureds.
3. Covering all activities everywhere, whether competition or sport, provided that the original suit for damages is brought in the United States of America.
4. Involving member-to-member as well as member-to-nonmember accidents.
5. Coverage is "excess" to any other applicable coverage.
6. Except first $50 deductible (property damage only).
7. Any AMA member whose model causes an accident should report the accident and file a claim when liability is incurred.

Claim forms and step-by-step procedures for filing a claim are available from AMA HQ. In emergencies, contact HQ. Phone: (703) 435-0750. Ask for the Insurance Claim Representative in the Special Services Department.

Persons and Activities Insured under the AMA Insurance Coverage Provided to Chartered Club/Chapters and Members Thereof

A. The following PERSONS—as to their liability for activities of the club/chapter or four activities performed on behalf of the club/chapter, as follows:

1. Any chartered club/chapter officer (each of whom must be an AMA member), while acting within the scope of this position and in the performance of his duties.

2. Any active dues-paying chartered club/chapter member (who must also be an AMA member), as defined in the official club/chapter charter or bylaws.
3 Any owner of property used by the club (when named by the club as additional insured) for any official activities (meetings, flying sessions, car races, boating events, rocket shoots, contests, etc.) for which the club is liable.
4 Any honorary chartered club member, defined as one who is not a dues-paying club member and who does not participate regularly in club activities; such member must be listed on the charter application as honorary.
5 Any associate chartered club member is usually defined as wife, husband, child or parent of an active club member who does not operate models as part of the club's activity; such member must be listed on the charter application as an associate.

B. For the following ACTIVITIES—as to the liability of the club/chapter for activities scheduled or designated by club/chapter officers as official club/chapter events, such as:

1. Any meeting of the charter club/chapter, indoors or outdoors, involving modeling or non-modeling activity, including club/chapter social and/or business affairs.
2. Any meet or contest sanctioned by the Academy of Model Aeronautics in which the club/chapter acts as sponsor and requires AMA membership of all contestants who participate by operating models.
3. Any model activity of the club/chapter provided that only AMA members are involved in operating models (aircraft, cars, boats, or rockets).
4. Any club/chapter involving guests to the extent that the club's/chapter's liability is protected for the action of any guest, but non-AMA member guests themselves are not insured.

Complete details of coverage(s) and exceptions are contained in master policies on file at AMA Headquarters, available for $1.00 per policy for handling and postage.

Appendix E

Academy of Model Aeronautics
Official Safety Code

January 1, 1984
Model Operations Must Be
in Accordance with This Code in
Order for AMA Liability Protection to Apply

General

1. I will not fly my model aircraft in competition or in the presence of spectators until it has been proven to be airworthy by having been previously, successfully flight tested.
2. I will not fly my model higher than approximately 400 feet within 3 miles of an airport with out notifying the airport operator. I will give right-of-way to, and avoid flying in the proximity of full-scale aircraft. Where necessary, an observer shall be utilized to supervise flying to avoid having models fly in the proximity of full-scale aircraft.
3. Where established, I will abide by the safety rules for the flying site I use, and I will not willfully and deliberately fly my models in a careless, reckless, and/or dangerous manner.

4. If my model weighs over 20 pounds, I will only fly it in accordance with paragraph 5 of this section of the AMA Safety Code, with a minimum separation of 65 feet between spectators and flight operations.
5. At air shows or model flying demonstrations, a single straight line must be established, one side of which is for flying, with the other side for spectators. Only those persons essential to the flight operations are to be permitted on the flying side of the line; all others must be on the spectator side. Flying over the spectator side of the line is prohibited, unless beyond the control of the pilot(s).

   The only exceptions which may be permitted to the single straight line requirement, under special circumstances involving consideration of site conditions and model size, weight, speed and power, must be jointly approved by the AMA President and the Executive Director. In any case, the maximum permissible weight of flying models is 55 pounds.

6. I will not fly my model unless it is identified with my name and address or AMA number on or in the model. NOTE: This does not apply to models flown indoors.

7. I will not operate models with metal-bladed propellers or with gaseous boosts, in which gases other than air at normal atmospheric pressure enter their internal combustion engine(s); nor will I operate models with extremely hazardous fuels; such as those containing tetranitromethane or hydrazine.

8. I will not operate models with pyrotechnics (any device that explodes, burns, or propels a projectile of any kind) including, but not limited to, rockets, explosive bombs dropped from models, smoke bombs, all explosive gases (such as hydrogen-filled balloons), ground mounted devices launching a projectile. The only exceptions permitted are rockets flown in accordance with the Safety Code of the National Association of Rocketry or those permanently attached (as per JATO use); also those items authorized for Air Show Team use as defined by the AST Advisory Committee (document available from AMA HQ).

NOTE: A model aircraft is defined as heavier-than-air craft with or without engine, not able to carry a human being.

Radio Control

1. I will have completed a successful radio equipment ground range check before the first flight of a new or repaired model.

2. I will not fly my model aircraft in the presence of spectators until I become a qualified flier, unless assisted by an experienced helper.

3. I will perform my initial turn after takeoff away from the pit, spectator, and parking areas, and I will not thereafter perform maneuvers, flights of any sort, or landing approaches over a pit, spectator, or parking area.

Free Flight

1. I will not launch my model aircraft unless at least 100 feet downwind of spectators and automobile parking.

2. I will not fly my model unless the launch area is clear of all persons except my mechanic and officials.

3. I will employ the use of an adequate device in flight to extinguish any fuses on the model after it has completed its function.

Control Line

1. I will subject my complete control system (including safety thong, where applicable) to an inspection and pull test prior to flying.

2. I will assure that my flying area is safely clear of all utility wires or poles.

3. I will assure that my flying area is safely clear of all nonessential participants and spectators before permitting my engine to be started.

Appendix F   Academy of Model Aeronautics

FREQUENCY IDENTIFICATION SYSTEM
EFFECTIVE JANUARY 1988

PLAN NOW!

72 MHz AIRCRAFT USE ONLY

Single **RED** streamer—7/8'' to 1'' wide by 8'' long affixed to the
top of the transmitter antenna imprinted with above wording

1988-1991 AIRCRAFT FREQUENCIES

Channel No.	Frequency	Channel No.	Frequency	Channel No.	Frequency	Channel No.	Frequency
12	72.030	24	72.270	38	72.550	48	72.750
14	72.070	26	72.310	40	72.590	50	72.790
16	72.110	28	72.350	42	72.630	52	72.830
18	72.150	30	72.390	44	72.670	54	72.870
20	72.190	32	72.430	46	72.710	56	72.910
22	72.230	34	72.470				

Channels 12-34 Narrow Band transmitter only   Channel 36 and 58 not used—see General Info

CHANNEL NUMBER PLAQUES

One and one-half inch **BLACK** numerals with 1/4'' stroke mounted on
a white background, visible on both sides of the plaque.

At modeler's option, they may read horizontally or vertically and be attached
at the base, center, or top of the antenna.

Non-reflective materials recommended.

GENERAL INFORMATION

Effective January 1988, channels 12 through 34 will be reserved for
narrow-band transmitters only. Older, broad band equipment, as well
as new narrow-band, can be operated on channels 38 through 56.

Channel 36 is not used in order to provide an 80 KHz spacing
between channels 34 and 38.

Channel 58 is not used to provide image response protection for
channel 12.

The channel usage and identification system is authorized for use in AMA sanctioned events and is highly recommended for all sport flying and club activities.

See pages 127-129 of the 1986-87 Official Model Aircraft Regulations for current frequency information and recommendations.

SEE OTHER SIDE FOR MORE INFORMATION

ACADEMY OF MODEL AERONAUTICS
1810 Samuel Morse Drive, Reston, VA 22090

FREQUENCY IDENTIFICATION SYSTEM

EFFECTIVE JANUARY 1988

PLAN NOW!

75 MHz SURFACE USE ONLY

Single **YELLOW** streamer—7/8'' to 1'' wide by 8'' long affixed to the
top of the transmitter antenna imprinted with above wording

1988-1991 SURFACE FREQUENCIES

Channel No.	Frequency	Channel No.	Frequency	Channel No.	Frequency
62	75.430	72	75.630	82	75.830
64	75.470	74	75.670	84	75.870
66	75.510	76	75.710	86	75.910
68	75.550	78	75.750	88	75.950
70	75.590	80	75.790	90	75.990

CHANNEL NUMBER PLAQUES

One and one-half inch **BLACK** numerals with 1/4'' stroke mounted on
a white background, visible on both sides of the plaque.

At modeler's option, they may read horizontally or vertically and be attached
at the base, center, or top of the antenna.

Non-reflective materials recommended.

OTHER BANDS

(Model Aircraft **or** Surface Models)

27 MHz

Single, colored streamer or triangular flag—7/8'' to 1'' by 8''

26.995	Brown	27.095	Orange	27.195	Green
27.045	Red	27.145	Yellow	27.255	Blue

6 METER

Amateur Radio License Required

50 MHz

Single, **BLACK** streamer 7/8'' to 1'' by 8'' and
channel marker plaque

Channel No.	Frequency
00	50.800
02	50.840
04	50.880
06	50.920
08	50.960

53 MHz

Two colored streamers 7/8'' to 1'' wide by 8'' long

Frequency	Colors	Frequency	Colors
53.100	Black-Brown	53.500	Black-Green
53.200	Black-Red	53.600	Black-Blue
53.300	Black-Orange	53.700	Black-Purple
53.400	Black-Yellow	53.800	Black-Gray

SEE OTHER SIDE FOR MORE INFORMATION

Appendix G

AMA District Frequency Coordinators

More information on radio interference problems can be obtained from these people. This list is current as of April 1987.

District 1: CT, ME, MA, NH, RI, VT
George Wilson
82 Frazier Way
Marston Mills, MA 02648

District 2: NY, NJ
George Myers
70 Froelich Farm Road
Hicksville, NY 11801

District 3: OH, PA, WV
James Bearden
5552 Foxrun Ct.
Cincinnati, OH 45239

District 4: DE, DC, MD, NC, VA
Paul Yacobucci
6408 Winthrop Dr.
Fayetteville, NC 28301

District 5: AL, FL, GA, MS, PR, SC, TN
Burnis Fields
P.O. Box 1063
Strickland Road
Interlachen, FL 32048

District 6: IL, IN, KY, MO
Loren Holm
3632 Main
Quincy, IL 62301

District 7: IA, MI, MN, WI
Bob Stamm
Box 357
Minoqua, WI 54548

District 8: AR, LA, NM, OK, TX
Scott Kalmus
814 West Centerville #125
Garland, TX 75041

District 9: CO, KS, NE, ND, SD, WY
Steve Mangles
Radio Service Center
918 S. Sheridan
Denver, CO 80226

District 10: AZ, CA, HI, NV, UT
George Steiner
2238 Rogue River Dr.
Sacramento, CA 95826

District 11: AK, ID, MT, OR, WA
Robert Balch
16439 SE Haig Dr.
Portland, OR 97236

Index

Edited by Steven H. Mesner